Mitch Murray's

ONE-LINERS
FOR
SPEECHES
ON
SPECIAL OCCASIONS

Mitch Murray's

ONE-LINERS
FOR
SPEECHES
ON
SPECIAL OCCASIONS

foulsham
LONDON • NEW YORK • TORONTO • SYDNEY

foulsham

The Publishing House, Bennetts Close, Cippenham,
Slough, Berkshire, SL1 5AP, England.

ISBN 0-572-02388-X

Cover photograph © The Image Bank

Edited by Carole Chapman

Printed in Great Britain by Creative Print & Design (Wales), Ebbw Vale

DEDICATION

This book is dedicated to my mother, Renée – who insists on embarrassing me by casually displaying my books on her coffee table.
I call her 'the doddery old broad'. She likes it. Go figure.

She shares this dedication with my late father, Eric – who was no slouch himself when it came to after-dinner speaking.
She liked him as well.

Names and characters in this book are used solely for the purpose of example. Any similarity between these fictional illustrations and real people is entirely coincidental.

So put that lawyer away and don't be silly!

Contents

How To Use This Book

It's probably not for me to say, but the great advantage with my books is that you don't have to read 'em, you only have to buy 'em, and you've already done that . . . so thanks.

You still here?

Oh well, while I'm waiting for the royalties to start coming in, I suppose the least I can do is give you a few tips on how best to utilise the material within these pages.

Here's the picture . . .

Imagine a Swedish smörgåsbord laid out before you – that's the book.

On the table are herrings, potato salad, anchovies, olive, beetroot, cucumber, pimentos, caviar and lots of other goodies – these are the one-liners.

Pick up your plate – that's your notepad.

Now, take only the goodies you fancy and arrange them on your plate – this is your speech.

Don't overload that plate, mate . . . it'll be indigestible.

Choose carefully, with taste and restraint or some of those items will come back to haunt you.

Okay. It's now time for me to abandon this analogy before it becomes ridiculous (what do you mean 'too late'?), and explain a few essentials.

- First of all, be aware that I'm using the term 'one-liners' in a very generalised way; sometimes you'll be using two- or three-line gags, sometimes the one-liner won't be funny at all – it could be a sentimental comment or a piece of prose.

- Start by looking for the category of speech you'll be making – Birthday, Retirement, Anniversary, Christening, Reunion etc. Make a note of the one-liners which appeal to you. If I haven't catered for the specific function at which your speech is to be made, chances are there's not much to say on that particular topic, so look for something similar.

- Sometimes, the individual categories will include suitable openers, sometimes they don't. Either way, your next move is to check out the Openers section and to select something witty and appropriate with which to begin your speech.

- Make a list of the people you'll be referring to, along with details of their occupations, appearance, personality traits, eccentricities and other qualities.
  Check out the corresponding one-liners and select one or two of the funniest for each of the characteristics you wish to highlight.
  Don't overdo it. You don't need to mention everybody present.

● Concentrate on the main subject of your speech and try to use the topic as a hub.

For example, in the case of a retirement speech, the 'subject' is the person retiring and the 'topic' is retirement.

The 'subject' of an anniversary speech is the couple and the 'topic' is their life together.

The 'subject' of a best man's speech is the bridegroom, the 'topic' is his marriage.

Have fun with the characters, but make frequent trips to the hub of the speech in order to keep it on track.

● As you list jokes about their little quirks or weird hobbies or social behaviour, keep one eye on that topic and look for opportunities to bounce some of these one-liners back to it.

In the case of the retiree, for instance, you could make fun of his disastrous attempts at 'home-improvement', then return to the topic by speculating on the havoc he will wreak now that he has so much more time on his hands.

In the anniversary speech, joke about the husband's endless golf jaunts over the years, then return to the topic by complimenting his long-suffering wife on handling the situation so well.

In the best man's speech, gloat at the curtailment of the bridegroom's former activities now that he's wearing a ring . . . through his nose. Once you have re-established the topic, you are free to wander back into one-liner land again, this time featuring a different issue.

● The lines you use should bridge to each other as naturally as possible with a logical pattern. I'd like to tell you more, but – hey, gimme a break – I've got to save *something* for my next book!

- Don't forget to browse through entertaining extras like Roasts and Insults, Absent Friends, Quips and Bits and Waffle.

- The important thing to remember about one-liners is that they have to have a ring of truth in order to be funny. These jokes are verbal caricatures. They take a defect or an idiosyncrasy and exaggerate it. Don't contrive an attribute or a situation in order to justify using a one-liner, no matter how funny you think it is. If a guy is of average build, don't try making 'fatty' jokes. You'll confuse your audience. If, however, he's obviously overweight, go ahead . . . make him as big as a house if you want to, providing he can take it and that you're sure the audience won't squirm with embarrassment on his behalf.

- Don't screw around too much with one-liners. Certain words which may appear innocuous or superfluous, could be part of the magic that makes us laugh. Removing those words, or changing their position may be fatal to the line.

- As you glance through the contents of this book, you may find that many of the lines need to be read out aloud before you see the joke. This illustrates how important it is to remember that you are writing for the *ear*, not the eye. Your audience will be listening, not reading.

- Don't ridicule women. Don't even *think* about it! Flatter them with positive humour or jokes which depict them as having the upper hand. Be extra careful about personal remarks or comments on appearance. If you ignore this warning and go ahead with risky gags about the fairer sex, don't come limping to me – I can't sew 'em back on for you!

● I don't recommend using cards for a one-liner based speech. At that pace, your frantic shuffling will distract and unnerve the audience. In any case, I think they look bloody poncey!

I suggest a full script, written on A5 paper, with about eight gags per page, clearly written in block capitals. Try my 'colourtext system'. This involves writing the script in varying colours: one gag in blue, the next in brown, then green, then black and so on. Underline the key words in red; this way, you won't lose your place so easily when you return to the text after looking around the audience.

Once you are familiar with the speech, the underlined words will often trigger your memory of the entire sequence, allowing you to look around the audience again. Very impressive. Trust me.

● Before you speak, establish where each of the characters you'll be featuring, is seated. Where their segment or mention appears on the script, draw a little arrow pointing towards his or her seating position. This enables you to direct your comments accurately towards the subject of your gag.

Brilliant, eh?

Well, that's what I'm paid for.

Enjoy the book.

ABSENT FRIENDS

Doug Fletcher was due to be here this evening, but I have to inform you that he wasn't able to come . . .
I *have* to inform you of that because otherwise, believe me, you'd never have noticed.

I don't want to spoil the fun, but I'm afraid I have to make a serious announcement . . .
I had a terrible shock when I heard this.
For those of you who have been wondering why Norman Pearson isn't here tonight, I'm very sad to have to tell you, our dear Norman has gone to a better place – the Savoy . . .

. . . stupid bastard, can't even read a simple invitation.

Alex Taylor apologises, he can't be with us this evening.
Domestic problems, I'm afraid.
A few weeks ago, he and his wife bought a water-bed and ever since then, they've been slowly drifting apart.

Our special guest this evening needs no introduction whatsoever . . . he didn't show up!

Duncan Bradley can't be here tonight. He's been admitted to Guy's Hospital for an emergency operation . . . they've had to remove a large breast from the palm of his hand!

Stan Pearce apologises, he can't be with us tonight . . . no one invited him.

Harry Fisher won't be coming along this evening; he couldn't make bail.

Gary Braden can't be with us tonight. Family reasons.
It says here, his grandmother is a *hundred and eleven* . . . isn't that wonderful?
(Possible applause)

. . . oh sorry, it's this bloody handwriting . . . his grandmother is *ill*!

Steve Weston can't be with us today; sadly, he's in a disturbed and confused state . . . California!

Noel Phillips couldn't make it tonight – but then, according to Elaine, he couldn't make it last night either . . .
or the night before . . . or the night before that.

Mike Bennett apologises, he can't be here; it's the baby's night off and he's got to look after the baby-sitter.

Jack Peters can't be here and I must say I miss him.
I always miss Jack – I'm a rotten shot!

Actually, I treasure every moment I don't see him.

Finally, Annie Crawford sends her apologies: she's trying to catch up with her male . . . lucky guy.

ACCIDENTS

Accidents will happen . . . we lose many, many people in this world through accidents.
On the other hand, quite a few people are also the *result* of accidents.

You may have noticed Andy Wilson's car parked outside. It's a very unusual vehicle . . . it has four headlights, two radiators, and the engine's in the back.
Of course it wasn't always like that . . . only since the accident.

There's been a freak accident at the junction of Shaftesbury Avenue and Tottenham Court Road . . . two freaks bumped into each other!

What a terrible accident! I had the right of way, but the other bloke had the truck!

Countless accidents are caused by two motorists aiming at the same pedestrian.

In America, most ambulance accidents happen when the vehicles are reversing . . . they keep colliding with lawyers.

Some time ago, he was with a new girlfriend and they had an accident in the car. Let me see, the baby would be about . . . eighteen months old by now.

He was once accused of sexual harassment. He was totally innocent. What happened was . . . his teeth accidentally fell into the fax machine, and – before he knew it – he'd bitten a secretary in Strathclyde!

My nephew just had a nasty accident. He was on his skateboard and he ran into a car . . . that Lada will never be the same again!

Last week, Charlie Rowland had a small collision . . . a thought struck him.

Every Sunday, since his skiing holiday, he likes to go out into the fresh air for a nice bracing limp.

Statistics prove that more accidents happen in the home than anywhere else, so drink up . . . what d'you want to go back *there* for?!

ACTORS

Our thoughts are with Simon Barrington tonight – quite a new challenge for him – he's playing Pinter at the Haymarket.
I've just been handed this note . . . (read from small piece of paper)
. . . apparently, Pinter's leading 5 frames to 4!

Simon was born in the theatre . . . in fact, it went down so well, his mother kept it in the act!

At his wedding, when the vicar said, 'Do you take this woman to be your lawful wedded wife?', he looked blank for a moment then shouted, 'Line?'

I saw his one-man show last night. If you ask me, it has too big a cast.

I remember the crowd outside the stage door shouting, 'We want Simon Barrington, we want Simon Barrington!'
You know, if someone hadn't called the police, they'd have got him as well!

His acting really moved the audience – everybody left at the intermission.

His performance made the whole audience cry . . . for their money back!

Simon has made so much money that at last he can finally afford something he's always needed . . . acting lessons!

He worked in films and tried to make a little extra on the side . . . but she didn't want to know.

It was a disaster movie . . . the script, the acting, the direction, the scenery . . .

He's been in so many turkeys, they've started calling him 'Paxo'.

He's got a stage name, a numbered off-shore bank account, an ex-directory 'phone and a car with black windows . . .

One day, an agent got him a job, but couldn't find him.

ADVENTURERS

WARNING: Please don't attempt these jokes in your own home unless supervised by a qualified humorist.

Martial Arts is all about restraint. My uncle was a Karate expert . . . he joined the army and the first time he saluted, he killed himself!

What a guy! Talk about stubborn. He died five years ago and he's still in denial!

He had a fabulous and exciting childhood . . . in fact, the circus ran away and joined *him*!

Then, of course, there was the time he was found on top of Snowdon . . . Princess Margaret was livid!

He came into the world as a man of adventure . . . The first thing he did when he was born was to bungee jump on the end of the umbilical chord!

He's a bit like 'Superman' – he's faster than a tall building and he can leap a speeding bullet!

I don't know if he believes in life after death, but the way he lives, you'd think he didn't believe in death after life!

He's so wild, cocaine sniffs *him*!

They don't come much tougher than him . . . when he goes ten-pin bowling, he bowls overarm!

I'm not really adventurous. Some people climb mountains because they're there . . . I've always avoided them for the same reason.

ADVICE

Those of us who need it most, like it least.

If you hit mid-life crisis and suddenly feel the need to 'find yourself', why not start with the Yellow Pages?
It could save you years.

Never buy a genuine Van Gogh from a guy in a Bond Mini Van.

The best way to stay young is eat right, exercise and lie about your age.

Never go out with a girl who is older than her bust size!

If you can tell the difference between good advice and bad advice, you don't need advice.

Always aim high . . . that way you won't splash your shoes.

Brother, if you have half a mind to get married, *do* it. That's all it takes!

A bird in the hand . . . is useless if you want to blow your nose!

Remember, never argue with a fool . . . he may be doing the same thing.

Always look out for Number One and be careful not to step in Number Two!

'There's nothing wrong with making love with the lights on . . .
just make sure the car door is closed.'
                                        (George Burns)

I'd like to end my speech with a piece of advice . . .
never end a speech with a piece of advice!

AGE

Some of these jokes are proof that the good don't die young.

Getting old works like this. First you forget names . . .
then you forget faces . . .
then you forget to pull your zip up . . .
then, you forget to pull your zip down!

Old age has one consolation; it doesn't last forever.

Poor guy; without mouth-to-mouth resuscitation, he'd have no sex life at all.

The silly old sod thinks he's such a street-wise big shot, he smokes Crack Phyllosan!

The best way to tell a woman's age is in a low whisper.

When a man has a birthday, he may try to take a day off.
When a woman has a birthday, she'll try to take five *years* off.

She claims that she's still thirty-nine years old. I can't understand it . . . when *I* was thirty-nine, it only lasted a year!

The age of fifty hit him so hard, he bounced all the way back to forty-three!

'You can live to be a hundred if you give up all the things that make you want to live to be a hundred.'   (Woody Allen)

Woody's relationship with Mia Farrow's stepdaughter, Soon-Yi, seems to be coming to an end. Woody's worried about the age-gap; it's not wide enough!

Brandy improves with age . . . the older I get, the better I like it.

You know you're getting old when someone compliments you on your snake-skin shoes . . . and you're barefoot!

The tabloids have started calling her 'Soft drink' because she'll go out with anyone from 7-up!

'I love younger men . . . they don't know what they're doing, but they can do it all night.'
                                                      (Joan Collins)

He's very old and very rich . . . the picture in his passport is by Rembrandt.

Thirty is a nice age for a woman . . . especially if she happens to be forty.

These three guys thought they looked like mature sex warriors . . . actually, they looked more like plain-clothes Chelsea Pensioners.

He just turned forty-five . . . he's just *turned* forty-five . . . he's really fifty-four!

(*See also* Birthdays, Retirement)

ANNIVERSARIES

YOURS

At first I wasn't really sure how we should celebrate the occasion . . .
I thought possibly, two minutes silence . . .
But in the end, we decided five hours noise would be a lot more fun.

Since the day we were married, I've tried never to wake up grumpy . . . I always let her sleep until I leave for work.

Shirley and I have a very well-balanced relationship . . . with us, everything's done on a fifty-fifty basis . . .
I tell her what to do, and she tells me where to go.

I really surprised Shirley on our anniversary last year . . .
I remembered it!

This really is a milestone . . . here I am, married for twenty-five years and still in love with the same woman . . .
If Shirley ever finds out, I'm dead!

'They call it a 'Pearl Wedding', because after thirty years together, you feel like stringing yourself up.'

(Don Maclean)

It's awful to grow old alone . . . Shirley hasn't had a birthday for eight years.

You know, from the very beginning of our life together, Shirley had me eating out of her hand . . . she'd do *anything* to avoid washing up!

. . . but, believe me, I simply couldn't ask for a better woman; if I did, she'd kill me!
Mind you, after this speech, she's probably going to kill me anyway.

THEIRS

They had fifteen wonderful years of total
happiness . . . then they got married.

I'll never forget that magic moment when he said,
'I do' . . . unfortunately, he said it immediately
after the vicar asked if anyone objected to the
marriage.

In the summer of '87, they were married, and
their daughter Christine was born six months
later . . .

(turn page other way up)

Oh sorry . . . nine months later!

Next year, he's celebrating his Silver Divorce.

Do you know what it means when you come
home at night to a woman who kisses you, sits
you down, pours you a drink and prepares a
delicious meal? Then she spoils you with love,
affection and tenderness . . .
Do you know what it means? It means you're in
the wrong house!

I've got another party next week . . . one of my
best friends has been happily married for twenty-
five years . . .
Okay, so it took him five marriages – so what?!

The best way to make sure you always remember your wedding anniversary is to forget it just once.

You know, I can't quite remember if this is his fourth anniversary with his third wife, or his third anniversary with his fourth wife.

Many people want to know the secret of their long marriage.
It's simple: they set aside time to go to a restaurant twice a week . . . a little candlelight, soft music and dancing.
She goes Tuesdays he goes Fridays!

A few years ago, on their tenth wedding anniversary, they revisited their original honeymoon hotel.
This time, *he* ran into the bathroom and cried!

They're a well-matched couple; she lies about her age, and he lies about the house!

Love grouts wrinkles.

TOAST: May you grow old together on one pillow.

BALD HEADS AND HAIRY WIGS

'The only thing that stops hair falling . . . is a floor.'
(Will Rogers)

If he'd stopped at five foot six, he'd have had no problem . . . Unfortunately, when he shot up to six foot, he went straight through his hair!

This guy is living proof that it's not only tough at the top, it's shiny too.

His hair has turned prematurely gone.

If he were a tyre, he'd be illegal!

He's got a receding hairline . . . it's receded all the way down to his arse!

You know, if there was such a thing as a Hair Fairy, Frank Stanton would be a much richer man today!

Frank is very upset and frustrated tonight; he spent forty minutes blow-drying his hair and then forgot to bring it with him!

Every week, he goes out looking for the perfect toupee. I call it his 'Hairtrek' . . . he baldly goes where no man has baldly gone before.

These days, most people try to put fibre into their diet. Frank Stanton likes to put fibre on top of his head!

I recently met the original owner of Frank Stanton's hair . . . it was on the Isle of Man, pulling a horse tram!

Why does he buy such cheap toupees? Now he's starting to lose hair that isn't even his!

I'll say this for him . . . that wig he's wearing makes him look twenty years sillier.

BARMITZVAHS

OPENING: Today, as our son Stephen makes that traditional Jewish journey from boyhood into manhood, Simone and I welcome you. We thank you for sharing with us the pride, the pleasure, the happiness and the joy . . . of course, if any of you would like to share the cost, we'd thank you even more!

Actually, we seriously considered flying the kid over to Las Vegas for a 'quickie' barmitzvah.

You may be interested to know that our family is descended from one of the lost tribes of Israel, the 'Samsonites' . . .
This was the tribe who wandered in the desert for forty years with very little food or water, but with really nice luggage!

Jewish mothers arrange their children's holidays . . . guilt trips!

Stephen is an only child . . . we decided to stop while we still outnumbered him!

He's a good looking young man now, but you should have seen him when he was a baby.
He was so ugly, at his circumcision, the rabbi crossed himself . . .

. . . Well, it's not easy to Star of David yourself!

As it happens, the rabbi did such a good job, I left a tip on the table.

Stephen, despite all the jokes, your mother and I really are very proud of you . . . not just today on your Barmitzvah, but every day.
You're hard working, conscientious and organised . . . my God, have we nothing in common?!

To our lovely daughter, Sophie, who may be feeling it's unfair that a Jewish boy gets all this attention at thirteen years old and the girl is overlooked, don't worry . . . when you're a couple of years older, I'll tell you all about something called a 'Briss'!

BASTARDS AND BITCHES

I'll never forget the time I first met Stan Pearce . . . and don't think I haven't tried!

The more I see him, the worse I like him!

Now I don't want to say he's an aggressive, arrogant, insensitive slob, but I'm just going to have to force myself . . . he's an aggressive, arrogant, insensitive slob!
Hey! That was much easier than I thought.

He was always a trouble-maker . . . when he was a kid, he even used to beat the crap out of his imaginary playmate!

There's something terribly wrong with Stan's heart . . . it keeps beating!

His idea of fun is going down to Eastbourne, knocking on the doors of elderly people and when they say, 'Who's there?', answering, 'Death! . . . are you decent?'

His idea of fun is sneaking into Claridges and putting piranha fish in the finger bowls!

His idea of fun is sneaking into the library at St. Dunstan's, and ironing out the Braille!

He's got a split personality . . . and I don't like either of them!

For my money, two people in this world really knew how to create tragedies: William Shakespeare . . . and Stan Pearce's mother!

They thought she had PMT, so the doctors ran some tests.
Turned out she *didn't* have it . . . she was just a bitch.

She's the kind of woman a fireman would carry *into* a burning building!

Lovely to look at, delightful to hold and heaven to kick.

She's the kind of girl any guy would be proud to take home to smother.

BIRTHDAYS

Dip into these segments and apply the most suitable to whichever birthday applies.

YOURS

21

Birthdays are nice to have, but when you think about it, too many of them will kill you!
Still, I'm too young to worry about that.

Of course, since the voting age was reduced to eighteen many years ago, there's no longer any real significance in being twenty-one, but we all love a good party and I'm really very grateful to Mum and Dad for their generosity, and for organising this one for me.

I consider myself a very lucky guy to have parents like these two . . .
They tell me that when I came into the world on this day twenty-one years ago, Mum and Dad were a little disappointed; they'd set their hearts on a golden retriever.

Apparently, I was *not* a pretty baby – mother
didn't get morning sickness until *after* I was born.

But they got used to me and it wasn't very long
before they started thinking up ideas to keep me
occupied and amused.
One day Mum and Dad decided to play hide and
seek with me . . .
three months later, I finally found them in a
house two hundred miles away in Aberystwyth!

But seriously, right the way through my
childhood, my parents were always there for me
. . . and, as you can see, nothing has changed, so
once again Mum and Dad, thanks for everything.

40

Actually, I would have been forty-*one* today, but
one of those years was spent in Leicester!

50

You know, age is a funny thing. A fit, young man
suddenly finds he's fifty years old . . . I just don't
get it . . .
Fifty! . . . Do you realise what that means?
I'm finally catching up with my IQ!

Fifty! . . . Any chance of half a telegram from the
Queen?

I've been told that fifty is the age when 'happy' and 'birthday' seem to go their separate ways.

Well, as far as I'm concerned, the figure of fifty is just a technicality . . .
I'm actually only forty-two plus VAT!

Still, I can't deny that I'm now well and truly middle-aged . . .
Middle-age has been defined as the first time you can't do it the second time.
Mind you, old age is much worse . . . that's the second time you can't do it the *first* time!

60

It's not such a big deal; Ronnie Corbett is sixty-*two* . . .
mind you, that's inches!

Of course, I realise the big 'Six O' may well be an important milestone in my life, but I certainly don't think of it as *old* . . .

I'll tell you what's old . . .

You know you're getting old when your birthday candles cost more than the cake!

That's old.

You know you're getting old when you wake up
to find your water-bed has burst . . .
then you remember you don't have a waterbed . . .

That's old.

You know you're getting old when you don't have
an enemy in the world, because they're all dead!

Come to think of it, what do *I* know about
growing old? I never did it before.

70

All in all, I suppose that being seventy is a bit of a
pain in the arse, but it does make you think. It
makes you think that . . . being seventy is a bit of
a pain in the arse!

80

What a relief! For the last three months I've been
saving up my breath to blow out those candles.

Do you realise that at eighty, there are six women
for every man . . . what a bloody stupid time to
get odds like that!

Let me assure you all that I'm determined to keep
very active for many years yet; I have no wish to
sit around listening to the sound of my own
arteries hardening!

The trouble with getting older is that what should stay down comes up, and what should stay up . . . goes down.

As many of you know, I never part with anything if I can help it, and I'm quite determined to hang on to my health as well . . .
Tonight, ladies and gentlemen, you've done me the honour of coming here to help me celebrate four score years . . . if only you were here to help me celebrate eight score draws!

(Important: *See also* Surprise Parties)

OTHER PEOPLE'S BIRTHDAYS

GENERAL

Ladies and gentlemen, Red Adair and his team are happy to announce that the candles on Stuart Reid's birthday cake are now under control.

To be given the opportunity of adding my birthday tribute to Stuart this evening, gives me an enormous amount of pleasure . . . maybe that'll give you some idea of how easily pleased *I* am!

When he was born, the world was in such a tragic state, he cried like a baby.

Culinary scientists have developed a new birthday cake . . . it's made entirely out of baked beans.
It tastes lousy, but it blows out its own candles.

We put candles on our birthday cakes to make light of our age.

TOAST: Here's to you. No matter how old you are, you don't look it.

TOAST: May you live to be a hundred years old, with one extra year to repent.

GRANDMA'S BIRTHDAY

You know, until quite recently, I honestly had no idea that grandma was anything like the age she is . . .
You certainly couldn't guess just by her appearance.
I suppose, the first time I began to suspect that she was much older than she looked, was the day she said she was hoping they'll raise the Titanic so she can get some of her things back.

You may have heard the old saying, 'God made grandmothers because he couldn't be everywhere'.
Well, my grandmother is a perfect example of that, and incidentally, if you *have* heard that saying, I'd be very surprised because I only made it up last night.

Grandma may be eighty years old, but she's
playing volleyball with the sun, and tennis with
the moon . . .

Grandma's having fun.

Long may the fun continue.

COMING OF AGE

Richard lives by his own special motto: work like
a dog, think like a fox, hump like a rabbit . . .
and . . . see your vet twice a year!
And boy, did I clean *that* one up!

He means a lot to me – he's like the son I never
wanted.

What a magnificent party this is, Richard is a
very lucky guy.
I mean, *my* family was so poor, they couldn't
afford to give me an eighteenth birthday party
until I was thirty-six!

I'm not kidding, we were really skint! For my
tenth birthday, Mum and Dad bought half a cake
with five candles and put it in front of a mirror!

It's not easy for me to pay tribute to this young man . . . he does it so much better himself . . .
To give you some idea, this morning Richard sent his mother a telemessage, congratulating her on *his* birthday!

Richard is an active member of the 'Young Farmers' Think Tank'. They all sit around, think for a bit . . . then they get tanked!

Of course, sometimes Richard has a little trouble remembering exactly what happened at some of the socials, and is never really sure how the hell he got home.
But, by and large, he isn't really a big drinker . . . it's just that he donated his body to Science and he's preserving it in alcohol until they need to use it!

Richard looks pretty solid, but in fact he's at the ideal weight for his age and sex . . .
Now I bet you didn't even *know* there was an ideal weight for sex!

Richard, I know for a fact, your parents are very proud of you and I do hope they realise this speech is all in fun. They're very protective . . . as a matter of fact, I'm not sure I like the way your mother's been looking at me and sharpening that knife, so I'd better wind this up and make way for some serious drinking.

Ladies and gentlemen, please join me in paying a sincere tribute to Richard Thompson on his coming of age, and a toast to what I'm certain will be a bright sparkling future.

Let's all raise our glasses to the birthday boy, and let us also include warm thanks to our host and hostess for a really super evening.
Ladies and gentlemen . . . to Richard and the Thompson family.

Good luck and happiness to you all.

WIFE'S BIRTHDAY

SELECTED LINES

You know, I'm sure that what Madeline really wanted for this birthday, was simply not to be reminded of it.
Well, please forgive me darling, but you don't get off as easily as that; you have to understand that I'm so proud of you I really couldn't resist marking the occasion in this way, even at the risk of being sent to the dog house, so you might as well sit back and enjoy it.

As I'm the man she married, for me to call her a perfectionist may sound a little immodest . . .
Well, actually, she's *not* a perfectionist! . . . she's much fussier than that!

Madeline eats her alphabet soup . . . in
alphabetical order!
It's a fascinating thing to watch . . . takes hours!

My wife is not in the least materialistic . . . the
only diamond she was ever interested in, was at
the end of a drill!
She really is a DIY fiend. At home, Madeline does
absolutely everything . . . and I do the rest!

When we were first married, and I was in a
romantic mood, I used to bring out the animal in
Madeline . . .
I remember, she'd run to the door and scratch to
get out!

As a homemaker, she was always so neat, tidy
and super-efficient that it nearly drove me nuts.
Once, in the middle of the night, I went into the
kitchen for a glass of water . . . when I got back,
the bed had been made!

I'm probably not the easiest person in the world
to live with – I have my peculiarities – but
Madeline certainly seems to know how to keep
me under control.
She's well aware that I sleep with my secretary
. . . mind you, Madeline *is* my secretary!

But in any case, my wife trusts me completely . . .
after all, do you think she gives our house keys to
just anyone?

FATHER'S BIRTHDAY

Here are some excerpts from a speech I wrote for a son paying a birthday tribute to his seventy-year-old father.

You can use ideas from this model and select appropriate one-liners from elsewhere in this book in order to craft your own speech.

Needless to say, the subject needn't be a seventy-year-old father . . . it could be a twenty-one-year-old brother, or a real mean low-down mother . . .

. . . or a woman.

Family and friends:

I've been given the honour of proposing this toast to a man who, over the years, has become almost like a father to me.

You know, there aren't too many people like our guest of honour; it's rare to find a man of three score years and ten who still wears Paddington Bear pyjamas . . .

with the hat and the little sunflower . . .

in the office!

As we all know, truth is stranger than fiction . . . Arthur Wood is stranger than both!

He's a remarkable gentleman . . . even at his age,
he's still quite capable of putting away five or six
pints a night . . . only prune juice, but . . .

Naturally he's beginning to get a few aches and
pains. These days, his *back* goes out more often
than *he* does!

But he really tries very hard to keep in shape. He
does fifty push-ups a day . . .
Not intentionally . . . he just falls down a lot!

He is, as we all know, a man of great charisma . . .
this guy could charm the knickers off a transvestite!

But it seems facile to describe my father as 'quite
a character'; he has a very complex personality
and in many ways, he's a paradox.
On the one hand, he likes to present himself as a
brash extrovert full of self-confidence with no
time for false humility.
Yet, at the same time, in his own way, he's really
very modest.

Now, it's difficult to spot this – takes a bit of
practice . . .
but he honestly doesn't take credit unless he
actually believes it's due.

Mostly, of course, he believes it's due.

And this modesty is shown in other ways; for
instance, when he makes a donation to charity he
does it quietly and anonymously . . .

He doesn't even sign the cheque!

No, he really is generous. Other people give perhaps one tenth of their income to charity . . . he does much better . . . he gives a twentieth!

Yes, he really has a heart of gold . . . mind you, so has a boiled egg!

But it's not for me to stand up here tonight and to tell you about all the great things he's done; he's almost certainly told you himself.

Instead, let me give you a glimpse of how this all started.
Allow me to take you back to the 19th of March 1923 . . .

In Munich, the Nazi party held its very first meeting, and a fresh-faced kid named Addie Hitler called for the repeal of the Treaty of Versailles . . .

In Moscow, Vladimir Lenin was stricken by a stroke and, thus struck lacked strength to struggle on as Soviet Supremo . . .

(Lick lips pointedly)

In Washington, President Harding announced his intention to run for a second term . . .

and while they were all too busy to notice, little Arthur Wood quietly sneaked into the world.

He was born at home . . . it wasn't until his mother *saw* him that she had to go to the hospital!

No, he was not pretty as a youngster . . . in fact, child molesters used to knock on the door and demand their sweets back.

But thankfully, he started to improve and by his teens he had become the fine figure of a man we're looking at tonight.

It was in his early twenties that my father made a major contribution to the world of medicine . . . he decided to stay out of it!

Dad has always set himself high standards.

As a young man, he decided that for his future partner in life, he needed a girl who didn't smoke, didn't drink, didn't drool over film stars like Clark Gable, and didn't keep asking for money for clothes.

When he finally found one . . . she was nine!

Luckily, it wasn't too long before the delightful Gwynneth came into his life.

Now, it must be said that my mother didn't realise what true happiness was until she married father . . . then . . . it was too bloody late!

Oh yes, ladies and gentlemen, by now, you've realised that this is not only my father's seventieth birthday, but it's also the seventieth birthday of most of these jokes!

Last week, one of mother's friends asked her,
'What are you getting for Arthur?'. Mum said,
'What are you offering?'

By all accounts, it's been a colourful seven decades,
but father has always led a good, clean life.
His only regret is . . . he's led a good, clean life!

Arthur Wood is now approaching those special
years, those golden years when you suddenly feel
you should be eating foods containing more
preservatives, because . . . well, every little helps.

One day, perhaps, he'll suddenly find he's able to
brush his teeth and whistle at the same time.

Never mind dad, the good news is that doctors
are now saying there's no reason why you
shouldn't enjoy sex past ninety . . .

as long as you let somebody else drive!

My father may be seventy years old, which is a
milestone, but *we* know that this man will always
be young.

Despite all his efforts, it's very hard not to love
Arthur Wood. He's a delight to know, and I'm
proud to call him my father and my friend.

So join me please, ladies and gentlemen, in
drinking a toast to a most remarkable man . . .

A real 'one off' . . .

Dad, we all wish you a very happy birthday, and many many more.

Cheers!

(*See also* Age)

BOOZE AND BOOZERS

And now for a man with a smile on his face, a song in his heart, and whiskey all down his shirt . . .

. . . a man who never touched alcohol, smoked cigars or chased women until he was nearly *eleven years old*!

He only drinks to pass the time . . . last night, he passed 1999!

At least he's a happy drinker – always laughing and shaking hands . . . even when he's alone!

He drinks something awful . . . I know – he let me try some.

When he offered to buy me a stiff drink, I certainly wasn't expecting an ice lolly!

He's only fulfilled when he's filled full!

This guy gets drunk on water . . . as well as on dry land!

Most of the time, he doesn't drink anything stronger than pop . . . mind you, Pop'll drink anything!

He drinks to forget . . . he drinks to forget that he's an alcoholic.

One night, he staggered up to a parking meter, put in fifty pence and the dial went to 60. He said, 'Blimey! How d'you like that? . . . I weigh an hour!'

He decided it was time to quit the drinking habit . . . he'd seen the writing on the floor.

I once had an Irish girlfriend who used to make illicit whiskey. For all her faults, I love her still.

At Honolulu airport, the welcoming Hawaiian girl had obviously been overdoing the Mai Tai cocktails . . . she barbecued a garland of flowers and hung a pig around my neck!

I don't really remember how I met Bridget . . .
I just sobered up one morning and there she was!

She once held up the launching of a ship for three
hours! . . . wouldn't let go of the bottle!

I proposed to her on my hands and knees . . . I
had to . . . she was under the table at the time.

After the party I took her home. Oh, it was so
romantic!
Her head was on my shoulder – someone else was
carrying her feet!

That was the night I realised Scotch is a soft
drink . . . three or four and it goes soft.

I've been on the Drinking Man's Diet . . . it's
great! I lost four days last week!

I'm a member of Alcoholics Anonymous; I still
drink, but under a different name!

I've been trying to be a bit more environmentally
friendly with my drinking these days . . . I've
already switched from regular Bacardi to Diesel.

You know, one of the best things you can do is to drink a lot when you get old. That way, every time you go to kick the bucket, you miss!

On this date, back in 1491, at 7.30am, Christopher Columbus discovered Trinidad. At 8.35, he discovered a cask of the local rum. By the following morning, he'd totally forgotten what happened the day before, and he had to discover Trinidad all over again.

He who drinks before he drives, is putting the quart before the hearse.

My uncle was a real hard man . . . I once saw him down two bottles of brandy and he didn't so much as stagger. Stagger? He couldn't even bloody *move*!

One day, he was so desperate, he drank a whole bottle of varnish.
He died, of course, but he had a lovely finish!

BORES

A speaker should be aware that nodding heads in an audience doesn't necessarily mean they're in agreement . . . they could be asleep.

Sidney Stafford is the type of guy who leaves no opinion unexpressed.

When he was a baby his mother dropped him on his tongue.

Sidney has agreed to say a few words this evening and, as we've only allocated an hour and a half for him, I think I'd better let him get on with it . . .

Thank you for your speech, Sidney – I enjoyed every week of it.

You were really on form . . . chloroform.

Every word of your speech was absolutely super . . . fluous!

Ladies and gentlemen, you may have noticed, when Sidney's in full flow, all I do is say 'Wow!' every now and then . . . it's not very clever, but it fits a yawn perfectly.

I may not agree with what he says, but I'll defend to the *death*, the right of somebody to shut him up!

He may have his faults, but as far as his children
are concerned, he's always there . . . always.
It really pisses them off.

BURNS' NIGHT

Burns' Night – January 25th – is a celebration of Scotland's most famous poet Robert Burns.
The menu nearly always includes 'Haggis, Neeps and Tatties' – a dish designed, no doubt, to keep the English away should the bagpipes not do the trick.
If all this fails, there are readings from Burns' poems and Scottish songs.

To comply with the very special etiquette of a Burns' Supper, all speeches made on the night should have a Burns theme.

Here are a few speech excerpts, along with bits and pieces you may find useful . . .

(Whew! Next time I sign a contract for a book like this, I must remember to read the small print!)

Ladies and gentlemen, you'll be relieved to hear
that I won't be speaking for too long tonight . . .
after all, wasn't it William Shakespeare who said,
'Brevity is the soul of wit'?
And wasn't it Shakespeare who went on to write
plays that lasted four and a half hours! . . .

Two-faced Tudor twit!

You never could trust Shakespeare. At least with Burns you knew where you stood!

In any case, up here, Shakespeare is regarded as being 'ethnically challenged'.

It's a strange thing with the Scots and the English . . . we have a differing viewpoint on almost everything; for example, Burns wrote, 'The healesome porritch, chief of Scotia's food!'

On the other hand, Samuel Johnson described oats as ' . . . a grain which in England is generally given to horses, but in Scotland supports the people.'

Most English people think that a Scotsman is a simple machine which turns beer into urine . . . most Scots think that English beer is urine already, and all that Englishmen do is recycle the stuff!

But, ladies and gentlemen, tonight is not the night to take the urine . . . my toast this evening is to the lassies, and that's one subject on which Englishmen and Scotsmen are united; we're brothers in bamboozlement, fraternal in flummoxation and kinsmen in confusion!
We love 'em but we know we'll never figure 'em out.

Rabbie Burns, whose track record with the lasses far outshone his aptitude for farming, was probably trying to reconcile these two differing talents when he wrote:

'O, gie me the lass that has acres o' charms,
 O, gie me the lass wi' the weel-stockit farms.'

I think I speak for all here when I say that we're
certainly surrounded by acres of charms tonight.

So gentlemen, please raise your glasses and join
me in drinking to the health, happiness and
eternal beauty of . . . the lassies!

It's my great pleasure tonight to respond, on
behalf of the guests, to the very warm toast
proposed by Archie Fraser.
I'm sure that Archie will understand if I seem to
be slightly overwhelmed this evening.
Here I am, a mere Englishman at a truly Scottish
event – a token Sassenach in a room full of caber-
tossers, a Burns Supper – a gathering in a mellow
mood. A throng, high on life itself.

When Robert Burns wrote 'The Holy Fair', he
must have been thinking about a crowd just like
this:

'There's some are fou o' love divine;
 There's some are fou o' brandy.'

Looking around the room, I think I'm ready to
announce the score so far: Brandy – 43 . . . Love
divine – nil.

Willie told me that when he first saw haggis, he
didn't know whether to kick it or eat it.
Once he'd eaten it, he wished he'd kicked it!

Ladies and gentlemen, I've only got three minutes left and I usually need that for applause . . . so let me close with some words written by – guess who – Robert Burns, who certainly knew how to appreciate the good things in life . . . good humour, good food, good wine, and *bad* women.

He wrote:

'A man may drink and no be drunk;
A man may fight and no be slain;
A man may kiss a bonnie lass,
and aye be welcome back again.'

To Ben McKenzie, and all our honoured guests, thank you for sharing the evening with us . . . you'll 'aye be welcome back again', any time!

—◆—

A little later, you'll be pleased to hear, Cameron Buchanan will be playing a selection of Jimmy Shand favourites on the stomach pump, but first, in the everlasting spirit of Rabbie Burns (a lover of all of life's pleasures – one of which, of course, is good rousing music) let us now savour the glorious sound that stirs the hearts of good Scotsmen everywhere . . . and frightens the holy shit out of their enemies!

So, lads and lasses . . . 'a skirl o' the pipes' from the Fraser Industries Pipe Band!

—◆—

TOAST:
'Long may your lum reek.'
(Translation: Long may your chimney smoke.)

—◆—

'The Kirkudbright Grace' (1790), also known as
'The Selkirk Grace':

Some have meat and cannot eat,
Some cannot eat that want it:
But we have meat and we can eat,
Sae let the Lord be thankit.

A FEW MORE QUOTES BY ROBERT BURNS
(1759-96)

If all else fails, drop one or two of these into your speech
and hope for the best.
Personally, I *still* don't see what all the fuss is about, but
then, I'm an East-Ender, ain't I?

'Partly wi' love o'ercome sae sair,
And partly she was drunk.'

'Gie me ae spark o' Nature's fire,
That's a' the learning I desire.'

'Leeze me on drink! it gi'es us mair
Than either school or college.'

'O thou! whatever title suit thee,
Auld Hornie, Satan, Nick, or Clootie.'

'Man's inhumanity to man
Makes countless thousands mourn!'

'Ae fond kiss, and then we sever;
Ae fareweel, and then for ever!'

Nope. Sorry. I *still* don't get it.

BUSINESS

When you speak at a social occasion, it normally matters very little whether the crowd remembers your words the next day, or forgets the whole thing.
The aftermath of a business speech, however, can be crucial.
Crucial to your product, to your company, or to your career.
In fact, the whole subject merits a book of its own.

Hey! I just remembered. I wrote one a couple a months ago – '*Mitch Murray's One-Liners For Business*'.
Tell you what . . . until you get hold of a copy, here are some lines to tide you over.

You know, participating in a convention of this calibre means a lot more to me than merely the strengthening of international ties, it means more than just prestige, more than acceptance by my peers . . . it means . . . a bloody great piss-up!

There'll be no talk, this evening, of budgets, financial targets or funding . . . this is a chance for us to forget trying to make both ends meet and to concentrate on making one end drink.

During the recession, things were so bad that even the people who never used to pay, stopped buying.

This man's a very unusual accountant; he has a life!

Three years ago, he made a major contribution to the world of banking . . . he retired.

In 1995, he became Deputy European Divisional Director.
Quite a thought, isn't it.
But then, of course, Dan Quayle was once Vice-President of the United States.
It's a funny old world.

Personal magnetism is that indefinable something that enables us to get by without ability.

I think the 'paperless office' is a bit of a pipe dream . . . it makes about as much sense as the 'foodless kitchen'.

I recently met a statistician's widow whose late husband drowned whilst crossing a stream with an average depth of three feet.

It's going to be quite a combination; a lawyer married to an accountant . . . they *had* to get married – it was the only way they could afford each other!
(or – lawyer/doctor etc.)

This man is a legend in his own CV.

Okay, so he's young, but look at his experience; since he's been with the company, he's gone through sales, marketing, planning, expansion, consolidation, reorganisation and now . . . puberty!

You know, the meek may well inherit the earth . . . but how the hell are they going to market it?

Our competitors, Clomco, have just held their own Achievement Awards ceremony . . . needless to say, nobody won anything.

He's subtle, understated and diplomatic. This is the man who once said to Sir John Harvey-Jones, 'Why don't you get a bloody haircut?!'

I just got a bill from one of our creditors, it said, 'Final Demand'.
Good! I was getting sick of their nagging.

Our chairman believes that 'yes men' are irritating, useless wimps . . . and I totally agree with him.

In this company, Donald Brown is looked upon as very much a father figure . . . you know, like Fred West.

Career woman: Someone who'd rather go out and be an employee, than stay home and be boss.

(*See also* Jobs)

CHARITY

'*May we strengthen the weak*
Give light to the blind
Clothe the naked
And be friends to mankind.'

I couldn't decide whether to help Save the Whale, Save the Rain Forests or Save the Children, so in the end I decided to save the money.

Next year we're planning a charity Chinese cookery demonstration . . . a 'Sponsored Wok'!

He sings for charity . . . if you've ever heard him sing, you'll realise he needs it!

Imelda Marcos did a lot to help Jewish charities . . . she planted thousands of shoe trees in Israel.

We were put on this earth to help others . . . but why are the others here?

He's a philanthropist . . . mind you, tonight he's more 'pist' than 'philanthro'.

Someone's got to take care of the homeless . . . you know, the homeless . . . Ex-Tory MPs!

'Money is like manure. If you spread it around, it can do a lot of good, but if you pile it up in one place, it stinks like hell!'

(Clint W. Murchison)

CHRISTENINGS

GENERAL

Maureen insisted on giving birth the natural way; no mascara, no lip gloss, no nail polish . . .

The baby looks just like his father . . . but so what? – as long as he's healthy!

This baby didn't come by way of a stork . . . it was all because of a lark.

Shortly after they were married, Maureen and Roy decided they'd like to start a family, and – sure enough – one day, came a blessed visit from that strange looking bird with the long, funny beak . . . her mother!

You probably didn't notice this, but earlier at the font the vicar held the baby in his arms and said, 'Now what are we going to call the little boy?' Jennifer said, 'It's not a little boy . . . you're holding my thumb!'

Actually, we were originally going to Christen our daughter Demi Bjork Ulrike Tootsie Marilyn Anneka Chelsea Paloma Goldie Madonna Robinson, but the vicar didn't have enough water . . .

Pity really, it would have looked ever so good in *Hello*.

Let's hope the baby inherits the best features from both parents . . . her looks . . . and *her* brains.

While the vicar was praying at the font with his eyes closed, little Timothy asked his mother, 'Why is that man talking in his sleep?'

The art of being a parent is sleeping when the baby isn't looking.

TOAST (BABY BOY):
A new life begun
Like father, like son.

TOAST (BABY GIRL):
Like one, like the other
Like daughter, like mother.

TWINS

I think one's a boy and one's a girl, but it may be the other way round.

You know, he shouldn't have started drinking so early in the day. When the vicar asked Roy what names they'd chosen for the twins, he said, 'Steak and Kidney'.
Luckily, Maureen stepped in, '*Kate* and *Sydney*, you pillock!'

CHRISTMAS AND NEW YEAR

Well, the party's off to a wild start . . . the ice is broken, and the way you're all drinking, the glasses will be next.

Taking your wife to a party like this is like going fishing with a gamekeeper . . . everything you catch, you have to throw back!

I'm sure by now, you've all had it up to here with turkeys, so you'll be pleased to hear that Pete Martin *won't* be speaking tonight . . .

Strange thing about Christmas . . . we leave homeless people on the street and we bring trees inside.

Why does Christmas always seems to come just as the shops are getting busy!

Did you hear about Santa Claus at Harrods? Seems he's been suffering from water on the knee . . . sometimes six or seven times a day!

My kids are at an awkward age; they're too old to believe in Santa Claus, and too young to believe in Liberal Democrats!

Last Christmas, Sally spent an hour and a half trying to stuff the turkey . . . Bloody hell, she nearly killed it.

Tough bird. It took nine hours to cook it! Every time we closed the oven, he blew out the pilot light.

By the way, if you need to thaw a Christmas turkey, thaw it with a chain thaw . . . it's *tho* much easier!

Here's a tip: Post your Christmas presents early. Give your friends plenty of time to reciprocate.

My sister in Melbourne sent me a boomerang for Christmas. As soon as I unwrapped it, it flew off back to Australia.

Her husband is one of Australia's leading geneticists. He's trying to cross a turkey with a kangaroo because he believes that the world needs a turkey you can stuff from the outside!

'Should auld acquaintance be forgot' . . . it could be the first sign of Alzheimer's!

My New Year's resolution: I've decided that, from now on, I'm going to learn to relax, even if I have to work at it twenty-four hours a day, seven days a week!

Sally and I have a little tradition . . . every New Year's Eve, I take her out and later, she brings me home.

By the way, when I said it was time to ring out the old and ring in the new, I didn't mean the year . . . I was talking about my socks!

TOASTS

Drink the brandy, stir the toddy
Merry Christmas everybody.

May your troubles in the coming year be as short-lived as your resolutions.

May you have a Christmas you won't forget . . . and a New Year's Eve you'll never remember!

CLOSINGS

An awful lot of rubbish is written about the closing of speeches.

In most cases, there's really no need for anything particularly clever.

Once you've said what you needed to say, you simply shove a full stop at the end of it and get the hell out of there.

People will love you for it.

Ten to twelve minutes of a snappy one-liner-based speech can be the equivalent of a thirty minute slow-paced talk. However brilliant your material and performance, there'll come a time when your audience has had enough. The laughter starts to lose its edge and you begin to sense the first stirrings of restlessness.

You have to pick up on this before it becomes a problem. Your instinct should tell you that it's time to wind-down. At that point, go straight to your closing section.

Go directly.

Do not pass 'Go'.

Do not collect £200.

Mark your 'retreat' point very clearly; I always draw a large red star at the top right-hand corner of the page containing the closing section. This ensures it's easy to find, should your audience go cold on you.

If your speech has more than one point to make, it's usually a good idea to run through these issues again just before you finish.

Make sure you have these headlines all in one place in case you have to break for the border, amigo.

Ladies and gentlemen, I have a great respect for the natural instinct of an audience.
It's staggering how, so often, they know a speech is over even before the speaker does. So, if you'll forgive me, I won't push my luck.

My horoscope this morning said, 'This is your lucky day – people will be so moved by your words and captivated by your charm and your wit, that they will rise to their feet at the end of your speech in a spontaneous standing ovation.'!
Ladies and gentlemen, I leave it to you – do you want to make a liar out of Mystic Meg?

. . . and Russell Grant too-oo-oo!

Now that we've all enjoyed a wonderful meal, I'd like to remind you that wild, uninhibited applause burns up twenty-five calories a minute! So start burning!

Cheers.

You know, the last time I spoke this long, my psychiatrist charged me £200, so I think I'll let you have your evening back.

I will treasure the memory of tonight until the day I die . . . or Tuesday, whichever comes first.

In conclusion, ladies and gentlemen, let us have a few moments silence in memory of the fourteen thousand prawns and two hundred chickens, who gave their lives to make this dinner possible!

Finally, I've been asked by the organisers to announce that, for reasons of safety, at the end of this talk you are requested to refrain from getting up on to the tables or chairs during my standing ovation.
Thank you for your co-operation.

If anyone here hasn't enjoyed the evening, would you kindly raise your hand . . . and smack yourself in the mouth!

Well, they say the best time to end a speech is when you feel the listening is lessening . . . so . . .

Ladies and gentlemen, I invite you to take glass in hand, rise to your feet and . . . just have a look where you've been sitting, 'cos I can't find the rest of my speech.
(Shuffle through papers frantically.)

Let me close with some words of wisdom from Professor John Cohen, Head of Psychology at Manchester University. He said,
'The man who first abused his fellows with swear-words instead of bashing their brains out with a club, should be counted among those who

laid the foundations of civilisation.'
You see? Here I stand – a pioneer of civilisation –
and you thought I was just being rude.
Never mind, ladies and gentlemen, I forgive you.
Thank you for listening.
Good night.

COUPLES

They had so much in common, they used to
spend hours together laughing at the same things
. . . his wife, her husband!

They were a fastidious couple . . . she was fast,
he was hideous!

What a pair! They do everything together; they
fight, they argue, they torment each other.

They married for better and for worse; he
couldn't have done better and she couldn't have
done worse!

They were happily married for two years: 1986
and 1991!

Stan is married to a wonderful person . . .
unfortunately, *she's* not that lucky!

I don't want to say it was a rough relationship
but their marriage counsellors were Frank Warren
and Don King!

He was stupid and she worked for Weight
Watchers . . . they stayed together through thick
and thin!

He was a dentist and she was a manicurist . . .
they were always fighting tooth and nail.

One night she had a terrible dream; she dreamed
her husband and George Clooney were fighting
over her, and her husband won!

As a couple, they have one main problem . . . he's
an early riser and she isn't.
He gets up early to avoid the traffic, and she gets
up late to avoid him!

They're looking forward to spending eternity
together . . . it's *now* they can't stand.

In her time, she's turned many a head . . . he's
turned many a stomach.

Two good, God-fearing remarkable people who
keep the Ten Commandments . . . five each!

But seriously, they're as happy as the next couple.
Unfortunately, the next couple is Charles and Di!

'One more word and I'm going back to mother.'
'Taxi!'

She could never leave him; she's spent too much
time training the bastard.

What a guy! He's given her everything credit can
buy!

They go together like Teflon and Velcro!

When he asked her to talk dirty to him, she began
to describe his fingernails.

They met when they were both having sex change
operations.

Like most couples, they have their little tiffs.
They had one just last week . . . nothing much
. . . two police cars.

DIVORCE

It all started back in the Garden of Eden when Adam's daughter-in-law divorced Cain because he wasn't Able.

When they first got married, everything was wonderful.
Then they left the church.

Some marriages are made in heaven and never fall apart . . . this marriage was made in Taiwan!

They married for better and for worse . . . but not for long!

If you're into statistics, consider this: a hundred per cent of all divorces begin with marriage!

It only takes a couple of words mumbled in church and you're married. It only takes a couple of words mumbled in your sleep, and you're divorced.

Jack and Hetty got a divorce after sixty-five years of marriage . . .
they would have done it sooner, but they waited for the children to die first.

A lot of people who marry, live happily ever after, but not until after the divorce.

At first she turned him on . . . then she turned on him.

It wasn't much of a marriage . . . 'for better, for worse, four months!'

You can sense your marriage may be in trouble when your wife starts lining the budgie's cage with your wedding pictures.

He was really stupid. One day she said, 'I'm leaving you!' . . . he said, 'Wait, I'll come with you'.

Their marriage was like the school curriculum. When they met, it was chemistry . . . then it turned to biology . . . now it's history!

Elizabeth Taylor says that she divorced her first, third, fifth and seventh husbands because they were odd.
(She divorced the others to get even.)

During the divorce negotiations, he came down with double pneumonia and his wife's lawyer demanded half of it!

Bachelor: a selfish, callous, undeserving man who has cheated some worthy woman out of a profitable divorce.

'You never realise how short a month is until you start paying alimony.'

(John Barrymore)

DOCTORS AND MEDICINE

I hope you enjoy my talk this evening; the last time I gave this lecture, it was to the British Haemorrhoid Society.
I got a standing ovation.

These days, doctors say that sex is perfectly all right after a heart attack . . . provided you close the ambulance door to stop yourself falling out!

Following their success with Dolly, the genetically-engineered sheep, Scottish scientists are now confident they can take the DNA from just one tiny piece of tissue, and clone an entire box of Kleenex!

Confucius he say: 'Man who buries head in sand becomes easy prey for determined proctologist!'

I eat so much fruit and vegetables that, honestly, if it turns out my body is short of fibre, I'll eat my hat!

I'm not a hypochondriac . . . I'm just a sick man in a perfectly healthy body.

I'm very happy to be here tonight . . . in fact, after that little operation, I'm happy to be anywhere!

You know, I really feel I fit in here . . . I fit in like a Penicillin Salesman fits in at a Christian Science convention.

I'm a bit worried about my doctor . . . last week, when I dropped my trousers for an injection, he dimmed the lights and started singing, 'Falling in love again'.

He has a remarkable reputation as a doctor . . . if ever you're at death's door, he's the one who'll pull you through.

If you've got trouble with your heartbeat, he'll soon put a stop to it.

He's a pretty cool character . . . his annual check-up takes a long time – they have to wait for his urine to thaw.

On their wedding night she said, 'Darling, I have a confession to make . . . I've got asthma'.
'Thank God!', he breathed, 'I thought you were hissing my performance!'

The only hot number he's into these days, is his blood pressure.

Things you don't want to hear during your vasectomy operation:
Number one: The word 'Whoops!'
Number two: 'Is it left over right or right over left for a reef knot?'
Number three: 'That reminds me, I must pick up one of those little red chilli peppers on the way home.'

Doctors now believe that if a man leads the lifestyle of a lorry driver, he's at greater risk of becoming HGV positive.

There's been a terrible epidemic up at the hospital wing of Durham Prison . . . three of the medical staff broke out with cold sores, four patients broke out with bed sores . . . and six prisoners broke out with hacksaws!

One thrush to another: 'Wouldn't you know it? I've got humans again!'

I'm half-Jewish and believe me, it's a very strange sight.

Charlie Rowland willed his brain to medical science. Five years ago, they came and picked it up!

This is the man who almost ruined a spectacular career in medicine by letting the air out of Mick Jagger's lips!

Patient: Doctor, I've started going deaf!
Doctor: No wonder, you've got a suppository in your ear!
Patient: Thank God! Now I remember where I put my hearing aid.

Ladies and gentlemen of the medical profession,   I leave you with this sincere wish; may your skills continue to help mankind, may your wisdom be to the benefit of all and, every now and then, may you inspire people to sit up and take notice . . . unless, of course, you're in the middle of an autopsy!

DO-IT-YOURSELF

I formed a strong attachment for my mother-in-law . . . and fitted it across her mouth.

Kevin has learned some valuable lessons . . . for instance, never again will he pick his nose while he's working with superglue!

Never again will he try to put the wallpaper on himself.
No . . . next time, he's going to put it on the wall!

He's so hopeless at do-it-yourself that last month a load of vandals broke in to his house, took one look . . . and re-decorated the place!

He's a real do-it-yourself freak . . . whenever anyone asks him for help he says, 'Do it yourself, freak'!

Tomorrow night, there's a celebration at Kevin's house; he's laid another tile! For him, DIY stands for – 'Do It For A Year'.

My vicar's very keen on 'DIT' – 'Do It Thyself'.

(*See also* Hobbies)
He never passed any exams at school, never did

EDUCATION

any coursework, never qualified for anything . . .
so, sadly, he'll never know what kind of work
he's out of.

He wasn't too bright. One day in the assembly
hall, he saw a sign saying 'Wet floor', so he *did*!

At the age of fifteen, he surprised everyone by
getting the school cert! What a dog *she* was!

He was a very sharp kid . . . he left grammar
school with ten 'O' levels and four 'A' levels.
Unfortunately for him, they caught him at the
gate and made him give them back to the pupils
they belonged to.

When he was seventeen, his father sent him
abroad to study.
Wow! He certainly learned a few things from her!

He received a Doctorate in History, but don't be
too impressed . . . in those days, nothing much
had happened yet!

He also studied Geography and liked to dabble in

American literature. He did papers on
Hemingway, Steinbeck, Thurber, Mark Twain . . .
and his brother 'Choo-choo' Twain.

I'll never understand metrication if I live to be a
gross!

All this talk about dyslexia . . . I don't even
believe the condition exists; I think it's a load of
carp!

I went to school with a tough bunch . . . ours was
the only class with a getaway car.

The dinner lady carried an AK47.

On school outings, we used to wear stocking
masks!

EGO

'*Most people who are as attractive, witty and intelligent as
I am, are usually conceited.*'

(Joan Rivers)

Thank you for that fabulous, enthusiastic reception but would you mind doing it again? My tape recorder wasn't on!

Tonight, I've been asked to talk to you about the importance of modesty – and I must say, you couldn't have chosen anyone better!

I went to Paris alone because I wanted to be with someone really special.

I'm enough to turn m'self queer y'know!

She really thought a lot of herself. When she was a nurse and she used to take a guy's pulse, she always subtracted five.

What an ego! When she has a climax, she screams out her own name!

He's lived with Shirley since 1989, and he feels really guilty about it . . . all these years he's been two-timing himself!

We'll never forget what he's done for this firm . . . we'll never forget because . . . he won't let us!

His prized possession is on his desk, inscribed 'To the greatest guy I know!' . . . and, let me tell you, I've never seen a mirror so well polished!

He came into the office and said, 'How's my favourite guy doing today?'
I said, 'You look fine to me'.

This character joined the Navy to let the world see *him*.

He once told me that if there's such a thing as reincarnation, he wants to come back as himself!

Some people marry for love, some people marry for lust, some people marry for companionship . . . Nick Webster did it because he wanted to see his name printed on match-book covers!

This couple is bound to be happy . . . they're both very much in love with the bridegroom!

I can see it now . . . every night, he'll take her in his arms, hold her close . . . and tell her how wonderful he is.

He thinks he's God's gift to women . . . if that's true, God does his shopping at Woolworth's!

They even wrote a book about him . . . 'The ego has landed'.

He's had loads of compliments this evening . . . two of them from other people.

EMCEE LINES
(Master of Ceremonies)

I have some good news and some bad news.
First the good news: Sidney Stafford is going to be making a speech later this evening . . .
That was the good news . . . and that'll give you some idea of how *bad* the bad news is!

By the way, Dermot Brannigan asked me to let you know that he couldn't be here in spirit, so he came in person.

I hear that Sidney's speech is going to be quite serious . . . there won't be any jokes.
Of course, with a suit like that, who needs jokes?

The gags that lie ahead of you tonight, are 'gags' only in the sense of what happens when you push a toothbrush too far down your throat!

Sam Dawson was due to be speaking this evening,
but a terrible thing happened on his way over . . .
he *got* here!

It's time now for our next speaker.
Unfettered by talent or technique . . . unhindered
by charm or personal magnetism, this man is in a
category of his own . . . *crap*!

Our next speaker is Graham Mayle, and I think
it's only fair to warn you, Graham is a bit long-
winded . . . in fact, he only sat down three days
ago from *last* year's speech.

Our next speaker is, by all accounts,
accomplished, inspiring, entertaining and a very
hard act to follow.
That's why I've made sure I'm going to be
speaking first.

Tonight has been like an acupuncturist
convention. One little prick after another.

Thank you Ed, your words were very moving . . .
in fact, you've made us almost pleased we invited
you.

The only thing better than a ten-minute speech
from this guy . . .
is a *two*-minute speech from this guy.

The last time Ed made a speech here, people complained about the PA system . . . they could hear every word.

It's always a delight to see a handsome man with a great speaking voice . . . maybe next year, we will.

ENGAGEMENTS

Hey! Whatever *happened* to engagements?
In my opinion, they're pretty useful; an engagement gives you something to break off. Without it, all you can do is to wait until you're married, then divorce.

Getting engaged was wildly romantic. The engagement party was a joyous indulgence.

Bring 'em back, I say.

Engagement: the period during which a girl decides whether or not she can do any better.

People are so impatient these days . . . in California, they've started fiancée-swapping.

He bought her a lovely engagement ring . . . it even had a setting on it ready for a real stone!

Just think of it, this time last year, Bob was footloose and fiancée free.

When I first met Joanne, she didn't have any teeth, so I bought her a set.
Then she broke off our engagement, but that wasn't what hurt me; I didn't like the way she laughed at me with my own teeth!

Most marriages follow a traditional pattern . . . first comes the engagement ring, then comes the wedding ring . . . then comes the suffer-ring!

You simply can't compare getting married to living with someone . . .
Getting married is a romantic commitment and a dramatic event.
Living with someone is when a relationship sort of fizzles in.

What a smoothie he was . . . his first words to her were, 'Is that an engagement ring? Well, ask your fiancé if he'd sell it to me and I'll leave it on your finger.'

He would never have married her but she piled on so much weight, he couldn't get his engagement ring off her finger.

ENTERTAINERS

Rod Bookman is a great entertainer and you know, to be a great entertainer, you've gotta have looks! He's got looks . . . you gotta have guts! He's got guts . . . you gotta have talent! . . . He's got guts!

Rod sings with his heart and his soul and with every fibre of his being . . . which is just as well 'cos he hasn't got much of a voice!

Last March, he packed out the Odeon, Hammersmith . . .
Mostly because he was appearing at the Shepherds Bush Empire.

He's the sort of entertainer who leaves his audiences gasping for less!

His show is so bad, they give you your money back on the way *in*!

He broke one of the strings on his guitar last week, but nobody will tell him which one it is.

Rod had a very nasty accident a few years back . . . he introduced Bill Wyman to a sixteen year old, and didn't get out of the way in time.

Touring is very hard on the woman in an entertainer's life . . . she just sits alone at home for weeks on end, while the singer is out travelling with his wife!

What can you say about Monty Maxwell? Anyone who thinks he isn't funny . . . has obviously seen his act!

Monty is the world's first sit-down comedian.

He went into comedy for all the right reasons. His philosophy was commendable; Monty believed that if he could make just one person laugh and enjoy themselves, his job will have been worthwhile.
That's exactly how it worked out – he made just one person laugh!

When Margarita Pracatan started singing 'Memories', Andrew Lloyd Webber walked on stage and personally crossed his name off the sheet music.

Poor girl . . . somehow, the TV cameras only seem to pick up her worst side . . . the *out*side!

Things are so bad in the circus business that even the elephants forget when they last had a booking!

Production companies are really cutting down on Pantomime costs. Next season, we'll be seeing 'Snow White and the Dwarf', 'Ali Baba and a Couple of Pickpockets' and 'Aladdin and his Torch'.

Even established TV performers are having a rough time. Things are so desperate, last week two soap stars jumped off Beachy Head, and Lenny Henry jumped off Dawn French.

FATTIES

Make jokes about fat folks *only* if you're sure they won't be embarrassed or upset.
Remember, people are allowed to make jokes against themselves, but this doesn't automatically give you the right to do the same thing.

On the other hand, if they're *that* fat, they probably can't catch you anyway.

Although I don't intend to make this a long speech, I think it would be useful for me to give you a couple of highlights from the life of our Guest of Honour – just a potted version . . . you know, something consistent with his belly.

We're talking about a man who is not only larger than life, but also larger than his own trousers!

The first time I met Phil Gorman, he was
standing on the corner of Oxford Street . . .
and High Street, Kensington.

Phil has the body of a twenty year old . . .
a twenty-year-old Volvo!

I don't want to say he's got a spare tyre but how
come he leaves tread marks on his girlfriend?

When Phil was born, he was so big the doctor
was afraid to slap him.

When he was a toddler, he couldn't play 'Hide
and Seek' – he was too tubby – all he could play
was 'Seek'.

He tried to run away from home once, but the
fridge was too heavy!

One day, his mother hung out a pair of his
Y-Fronts to dry, and a family of New Age
Travellers moved in.

During his holiday in Spain, he held his stomach
in so much he put his back out.

The doctor said he has to watch his waistline.
Shouldn't be too hard; it's right out there in front
where he can see it.

Don't sit next to him when he's eating . . .　you
might get 'passive fat'!

As it happens, he's very conscious of his diet.
Every day he tries to eat something from one of
the four main food groups . . . McDonalds,
Burger King, Wimpy and Kentucky Fried
Chicken!

Scientific researchers have come up with a
foolproof contraceptive for people over fifteen
stone in weight . . . nudity!

My friend Jerry saw a picture of Pamela
Anderson, measuring 38-23-35, and suddenly
realised what's wrong with his wife . . .
she's inside out!

She's wonderful in the kitchen – chicken, turkey,
salmon.
You name it – she'll eat it!

She's eating for two . . . herself and Newcastle-
upon-Tyne!

She's svelte . . . she's svelte to double the size she vas.

She has so many chins, she has to use a bookmark to find her necklace!

I hesitate to say she's fat, but how come nobody leaves the Opera House until she sings?

Recently, when she sat down to rest in a second-hand car lot, they painted a price on her glasses.

FOOD AND COOKING

I wrote a microwave cookbook once . . . the whole thing took me three minutes, forty-five seconds.

Last night, my wife had a nasty accident in the kitchen . . . dinner!

I knew I had trouble the first time I asked her for an aspirin and a glass of water, and she had to 'phone her mother for the recipe!

Her cooking leaves a little to be desired . . . namely – taste!

She's not an expert cook . . . the other day she boiled an egg for twenty minutes, and it *still* didn't go soft.

. . . but I miss my wife's cooking . . . as often as I can!

Yesterday I had a cup of tea with two lumps . . . my wife and her mother.

Her cooking really is awful. The first time she made me alphabet soup, I spelled out 'Help!'

Mind you, they do say that a bowl of alphabet soup a day, is good for the vowels!

Her speciality is that famous Greek dish: 'Gastro-enteritis.'

She's a graduate of the Karate School of Cookery – she was trained to kill with a single chop!

Normally, I hate to eat and run, but with her cooking, I have no choice.

She prepares dishes no one can face . . . in the summer, the flies come in, look at what she's done, and swat themselves!

If we want to punish the kids, we send them up to bed *with* dinner.

She used to dress to kill . . . now she just cooks that way.

I'm worried . . . we had people over for dinner two weeks ago and they're still sitting there!

In the USA, they shove religion at you wherever you are. I was in a restaurant in Atlanta and found myself being served by Jehovah's Waitresses!

The southern part of the Caspian Sea produces 'Beleaguer Caviar' . . . that's where Russian trawlermen surround a sturgeon and force it to surrender its eggs.

As they used to say in darkest Africa, 'He who hesitates is lunch!'

FUNERALS AND WAKES
(Yes, really)

If you are ever called upon to deliver a eulogy, the tone of your speech should depend very much upon the age of the deceased and the circumstances of their death. Your function is to comfort close friends and family members without resorting to excruciating platitudes or clichés. There is often a place in a eulogy for some gentle and respectful humour, particularly if the deceased happened to be a bit of a character. Relate one or two light-hearted anecdotes if you can, and close on an inspiring, positive message.

The following, although not exactly one-liners, may nevertheless be of some use at funerals and wakes. After all, let's be honest, you do have to be a little stiff to appreciate them.

To be born a gentleman is an accident –
To die one is an accomplishment.

'Oh here's to other meetings,
And merry greetings then,
And here's to those we've drunk with,
But never can again.'

(Stephen Decatur)

We come into this world naked and bare,
We go through this world with sorrow and care,
We go out of this world, we know not where,
But if we're good fellows here, we'll be
thoroughbreds there.

'I am ready to meet my maker. Whether my
maker is prepared for the great ordeal of meeting
me is another matter.'

(Sir Winston Churchill)

Sympathy is thinking with your heart.

You can't control the length of your life, but you can control its breadth, depth and height.

'He first deceased; she for a little tried
To live without him, liked it not, and died.'
(Sir Henry Wotton)

AN IRISH TOAST: Let not the devil hear of his death till he's safe inside the walls of Heaven.

Here are some more lines connected with funerals and wakes.
Don't use these on the day, unless you have a very cool crowd indeed.

What an organiser he was. If he'd have been running this funeral, we'd have all been down the pub by now.

I can let you into a little secret. His will reads, 'Being of sound mind, I spent all my money'!

I've decided to have my body preserved in a Cryogenic chamber . . . I'm also going to have my assets frozen at the same time so I won't be skint when they thaw me out.

Of course there's life after death; you don't think we get off *that* easy do you?!

Mark Twain's choice of the ideal afterlife: 'Heaven for the climate, Hell for the company'.

Epitaph for an Atheist: 'All dressed up and no place to go'.

Funeral director: 'Do you want your mother-in-law buried or cremated?'
Client: 'Let's not take any chances, let's do both.'

This was a very patriotic man. He was so patriotic that we couldn't risk letting the organist play the National Anthem!

'The graveyards are full of people the world couldn't do without.'

(Elbert Hubbard)

We're now going to hear a few words from Sean, who today is a bit like our dear departed friend over there . . . he's necessary for the party, but nobody expects him to say too much.

Temptation: A ventriloquist at a funeral.

I passed by a funeral the other day. It was impressive; two shiny hearses and right behind them, a man with a mad vicious dog. All this was followed by a procession of more than a hundred men.

I asked the mourner, 'What's the story behind this?' The man with the dog said, 'That's my wife and mother-in-law in the coffins . . . my dog bit them!'

I said, 'Can I borrow the dog?' The bloke said, 'Get in line!'

GARDENING

Just remember – an hour of rain can do more for your lawn in ten minutes, than a month of watering can do in a week.

He *loves* gardening. He puts on a floppy hat, old clothes, holds a trowel in one hand and a lager in the other and goes out to tell the man where to dig.

He's got green fingers . . . he's not a great gardener, he's just a messy painter!

He used to grow Bonsai trees as a business . . . his company became so successful, they had to move into smaller premises.

When it comes to my garden, everything's coming up roses . . . unfortunately, I planted tomatoes.

Last month I put in a rock garden. Two of the rocks died!

In Manchester, we get so much rain, I don't mow my lawn . . . I stir it!

Did you hear about the tree doctor who fell out of his patient?

The sight of my garden is enough to make a vegetarian go back to meat.

No gardener will ever understand why Noah loaded those two slugs onto the ark!

What a gardener! This guy could plant feathers and grow Kentucky Fried Chicken!

He's a little obsessive . . . he not only waters his lawn, he blows it dry and styles it!

Sometimes he gets carried away though . . . he got into trouble with Belinda recently when he pruned her dog.

He's a very keen gardener, our vicar . . . he put a sign up outside the church, 'Keep off the grass. This means thou!'

GAYS

What can you say about a guy whose bathroom towels are marked 'His' and 'His'?

A fellow whose father looks upon him as the son he never had.

Yes, Dennis is a wonderful, gentle, sweet man . . . he wouldn't hurt a fly. Unless it was open!

But you just can't *buy* friends like Dennis . . . except in certain bars in San Francisco.

He's the only guy I know who walks with a lisp!

He's very keen on drag racing . . . and let's face it, it can't be easy jumping hurdles in a cocktail dress!

He has a real flair for languages . . . on his very first day in Athens, he picked up a little Greek!

One day he passed a recruiting office with a large sign in the window, 'The Royal Marines Build Men!'
He walked in and ordered six!

He's a raving homo . . . wner.

Actually, he's bi-sexual . . . he likes men *and* boys!

But I'm sure that one day, he'll meet the right girl . . . and ignore her.

You can't offend this man no matter how rude you are . . . to him, 'up yours!' is a great offer!

He buys all his clothes at a little shop in Chelsea, 'Boys R Us'.

You know, this old-timer was a pretty wild dancer back in the forties. He was an expert at bebop, swing and jitterbuggering.

Should a couple embarking on marriage be frank and earnest?
Or should one of them be a girl?

His date was pretty, there's no doubt about that – but there was no getting away from the fact that her name was Kevin and she was a plasterer.

But he's perfectly normal, even though she doesn't look it!

You know what they say . . . three times a bridesmaid, never a groom.

GOLD-DIGGERS

Is it love, or is it fiscal attraction?

She has what it takes to take what he has.

She genuinely loves him for what he is . . . rich!

Her idea of 'quality time' . . . is a Rolex.

She's very keen on winter sports . . . especially if the old bastards have got lots of money!

We held hands all evening . . . we *had* to hold hands; it was the only way to keep her away from my wallet.

She really likes the good things in life . . . I don't know if you overheard this, but earlier, when the vicar asked if there were any objections, Lucy said, 'Yeah! What's all that crap about 'for richer or for poorer'?'!

We still keep in touch . . . last month, it was £100 touch.

She's really going to have to stop spending the kind of money she'd been spending . . . mine!

We had an open marriage . . . my wallet.

Every night, she'd go over to his place, sit with him, and gently run her fingers through his money.

It's an ideal marriage – she's the treasure, and he's the treasury!

Some men marry poor women to settle down . . . he married a rich woman to settle up.

He loved her so much, he worshipped the very ground her father developed a hundred and twenty luxury homes on.

Many a man is looking for a mature woman with a strong will . . . made out to him!

He's just had some bad news about his rich old uncle . . . he's getting better!

Strange the way they met . . . he just opened his wallet, and there she was.

GOLF DINNERS

'There's definitely a connection between pain and pleasure – golf spelled backwards is 'flog'.'
(Phyllis Diller)

Ladies and gentlemen, I don't propose to beat around the bush this evening . . .
We had quite enough of that out on the course today.

There's an old saying: 'After the age of fifty, golf takes the place of sex.' If that's the case, I'm going to assume none of you are in a particular hurry to get home tonight, and I'll pace my speech accordingly.

G.O.L.F: Great opportunity to look foolish.

They called it 'golf' because all the other four-letter words were taken.

My wife said if I didn't give up golf, she'd leave me! You know, I'm really going to miss her!

'Golf is like a love affair . . . if you don't take it seriously, it's no fun; if you *do* take it seriously, it breaks your heart.'

(Arnold Daly)

Golf is like sex . . . you always think you're going to do better next time!

I should never have taken my bank manager golfing with me . . . every time I yelled 'Fore!', the banker yelled 'Closure!'

It'll be a sad time for Wentworth, the day John Goodbar leaves the club . . . the neighbours'll have to start buying their own golf balls.

His golf style has to be seen to be believed . . . I have, and I don't.

It takes a lot of balls to play golf the way he does!

When Bob Graham began learning golf, he said that he'd move heaven and earth to play the game properly.
Well, he's only got heaven to move now!

Arnie Foster's doctor advised against playing golf . . . he said that at his age, he shouldn't risk getting so close to a hole in the ground.

Arnie's golf game is like his sex life . . . he only plays a round a few times a year and even then, he has trouble finding partners!

In my opinion, it's impossible to praise Arnie's golfing abilities too highly;
it's impossible to praise them at all . . . he's crap!

Mind you, he's never lost a ball . . . he's never hit it far enough to lose it!

You know, I think I've finally figured out the game . . .
• If it goes to the right, it's a slice
• If it goes left, it's a hook
• And if it goes straight . . . it's a bloody miracle!

I played golf yesterday and shot a birdie. I was trying to putt and the little bastard wouldn't stop tweeting!

HECKLERS

Night Club comics often have to cope with loudmouth drunks and various nasty customers. The professional comedian is usually well-armed with several lines designed to turn the tables on the smart-arse and to get an extra laugh or two at the heckler's expense.

At a private social occasion, however, any heckling is usually very good-natured and restrained. It would be rather heavy-handed, if not churlish, for a social speaker to learn professional anti-heckler lines simply for the purpose of silencing someone enjoying the party.

So here they are . . .

> **This man believes he's a wit and as it happens, he's half right!**

> **Would you mind turning round? I hate to laugh in your face!**

> **Feel free to speak your mind . . . I have a spare three seconds.**

> **You know, you really shouldn't drink on an empty head!**

> **Nice to see your voice is working. Shame it's not connected to anything.**

Isn't she a treasure? I wonder who dug her up.

Well, if it isn't Joanna Lumley . . . and it isn't.

Look! A bombed blondshell.

Hey! I thought alcoholics were meant to be anonymous!

Is there a new life form out there that we don't yet know about?

He may *look* stupid, but that doesn't mean he's not!

Look at him! Maybe we can freeze him until they find a cure!

One more outburst like that and you'll never deliver pizza in this town again!

I'm getting paid to act like a prick . . . what's *your* excuse?

Would you mind keeping it down in the cocaine section, please?

Carry on like this and I won't get to the funny stuff!

HOBBIES

Last June, he joined a bridge club . . . he was one of the first to jump.

I was thinking of getting a catamaran, but then I thought, 'Naah . . . two hull with it!'

When he goes fishing, the fish go home and boast about the size of the bait they stole.

Let's be honest, he's not much of a fisherman . . . if there was an epidemic, he'd be lucky to catch one measle!

He once built a ship in a bottle . . . we had to break the bottle to get the poor bugger out.

Another time, he tried to fix a cuckoo clock. Now it backs out and says, 'What time is it?'

I read a lot but I don't think much of it really sinks in . . . most of the time, it just goes in one eye and out the other.

I just spent an hour and a half on the Nordic Track
. . . one more hour and I'll have assembled it.

One of his hobbies is painting. He specialises in
still life.
He might like to try painting my wife sometime.

(*See also* Do-It-Yourself, Sport)

HOLIDAYS

The pool was so crowded, I had to dive in three
times before I hit the water.

I don't need a holiday this year, I'm broke already.

Try Las Vegas for a holiday; you can't beat the
weather, the entertainment, or the odds!

I've got two weeks to live; my wife's on holiday!

One way to keep your holiday memories alive for
months and months, is to use your MasterCard.

Half way through her holiday, she sent her
psychotherapist a post card: 'Having a wonderful
time . . . why?'

The planes were running so late, we passed Glenn Miller flying across the Channel!

What a lousy hotel . . . I was a prisoner of the Viet Cong for three years and I had a better room!

He didn't say he was taking her to Florida, he said he was going to Tampa with her!

They're going to Marbella in June . . . God knows how Phil's going to hold his stomach in for two solid weeks.

There were so many topless girls on the beach, it took a physiotherapist three weeks to unwind my neck!

JOBS

Every Friday he takes his salary to the bank . . . he has to take it; it's too little to go by itself!

You can always depend on an undertaker . . . he'll be the last person to let you down.

He's a tax inspector – from the tips of his cape to the blood on his fangs!

He was going to be a priest, but he kept giggling during the last rites.

In his early twenties, he became a police reporter . . . twice a week he had to report to the police.

What a useless reporter! The only decent scoop he ever got, was Rum 'n' Raisin, down at Haagen-Daz!

He's a book-keeper . . . I should know, I lent him one once.

As an accountant, he's very well respected . . . in fact, he's a ledger in his own lifetime.

I'm going to have to dump that girl who works at the bank.
Too risky! I've just heard she's a teller!

He's an alternative garage mechanic . . . he uses acupuncture to repair your tyres.

When he started up in the motor trade, most of his cars wouldn't!

Don't ever ask directions from a postman . . .
I tried it once. He said, 'Go straight down until
you get to WC1 3AJ, turn left at WC4 8RS, left
again at EC5 1JP and make a right into EC2
3BT.'

She makes a pretty good living selling eyebrow
tweezers to Noel and Liam Gallagher!

Farming is in his blood. Once, when Richard
hinted he'd like to go down and work in London,
Len tried to convince him to carry on the family
tradition.
I remember he said at the time, 'You should stay
here my lad . . . till the soil!'
Richard said, 'Till the soil does what?'!

Being a farmer, Richard is a real animal lover, but
I'd like to make it quite clear that so far, he hasn't
been charged with any offence!

. . . mind you, nobody's really sure why he
recently became the only farmer in history ever to
have been slapped round the face by a sheep!
I can't understand it, I saw that sheep and
between you and me, it was a bit of a dog.

As we dentists say: 'A plaque on all your houses!'

If a dentist breaks a dental mirror in your mouth,
do you get seven years of bad teeth?
Of course, a good lawyer will get it down to five.

I'm not very impressed with reincarnation . . .
I had this bloody job last time!

KIDS

So many kids these days are subjected to questionable
influences and bad company . . . but then, you can hardly
stop them mixing with their own parents, can you?

I was a very naughty kid. I was spanked so much,
I ended up with a cauliflower arse!

The most dangerous game we used to play at
school was bubble gum roulette . . . six kids burst
their bubbles in your face and one of them had
the mumps!

My wife and I were never blessed with kids . . .
although we've had three.

Lucy was full of energy and vitality from the very
beginning . . . even when she was just a few
weeks old, she was the life and soul of the potty.

One day she ran away from home, but for three years nobody missed her – we all thought she was still in the bathroom!

Not too long ago, Tony Blair caused a bit of controversy when he admitted that, occasionally, he used to smack his children.
Well I must confess – so did I.
To this day I still don't know why; after all, Tony Blair's children never did *me* any harm.

People with no children are really missing out . . . they'll never know what a thrill it is to come home after a hard day, sit down to a hot dinner and watch someone stuffing Spaghetti Hoops up their nose!

Kids are crucial to family life . . . without them, how the hell would we ever be able to program a video recorder?!

We have only one child, but then Hiroshima had only one bomb!

At kindergarten he was different from all the other five-year-olds . . . he was eleven!

At the moment, he's working his way through reform school.

Stan Pearce is an obsessive workaholic. His wife complained, 'The kids hardly see you any more!' He said, 'Kids?'

When little Tim was born, his mother cradled him in her arms and said to his father, 'Well Paddy, what do you think we should call it?' Paddy took one look at the baby and said, 'Quits'.

Some people say children should be seen and not heard.
I disagree . . . why the hell should they be seen.

LAWYERS AND THE LAW

The best things in life are fees.

William Shakespeare wrote: 'Let's kill all the lawyers', and bear in mind this was long before the OJ Simpson case.

The ideal legal client is a very wealthy man in deep shit!

In the United States, two people out of five regularly use lawyers . . . the other three *are* lawyers.

My lawyer is one of the new microwave lawyers
. . . you spend eight minutes in his office, and get
billed as if you'd been there eight hours.

Question: What's the difference between a lawyer
and an arrogant rooster?
Answer: The rooster clucks defiance.

Question: Why are lawyers like sperm cells?
Answer: Only one in a thousand has the chance
of becoming a real human being.

Question: What's brown and black and looks
good on a lawyer?
Answer: A rottweiler.

When Gerry Marshall was a kid, his burning
desire was to become a pirate. Now, he's a lawyer.
He's lucky; very few people realise their ambition.

You know, I never realised how many lousy
lawyers there are in this country until I visited
Pentonville.

I once had a little talking bird that used to lie
under oath . . . a perjurygar!

Why is it that every time a witness offers to tell
the whole truth, some lawyer objects?

LAZY BONES

My parents were hard-working people . . . they used to get up every morning at 5.30, do sixteen hours of strenuous work, and thought nothing of it. I'm the same way . . . I don't think much of it either.

Danny Webb is not the type of guy who sits watching the clock, waiting for half past five . . . he leaves at four!

He's not lazy exactly; it's just that he likes to relax over a cup of coffee . . . sometimes for three or four months.

When it comes to hard work, this man knows no fear . . . ask him to do some and he'll say, 'No fear!'

Danny is a shift worker . . . any time someone mentions work, he shifts!

He doesn't like working on Wednesdays, it screws up both weekends.

For this man, 'Trivial Pursuit' is not a board game – it's his lifestyle!

He hates mornings . . . they're so early.

He's certainly not obsessed with the need to be punctual. He's found that when you get to work on time, it makes the day much too long.

Some guys go bird-watching for a hobby . . . Danny Webb prefers lying in a hammock, letting the birds watch *him*.

He was always a bit of a couch potato. Even back in the sixties, when everybody else tuned in, turned on and dropped out, he used to tune out, turn in and drop off!

He simply can't bear to watch his wife doing all that heavy work in the garden . . . so he draws the curtains.

At least he helps to clean the house . . . he sits in front of the TV and gathers dust.

Next week he's going into hospital to have something removed from his arse . . . a chair!

LOSERS

'Life has its ups and downs you know,
That's nature's wicked rub
So if at first you don't succeed,
Welcome to the club!'

(Too modest to attribute.)

He's so unlucky. It all started when he went to a funeral and caught the bouquet!

It's pathetic; he once asked his local librarian to trace his roots . . . she discovered that his great grandfather had an overdue book, and made him pay the fine!

Some guys have 'savoir faire' . . . this guy doesn't even have bus fare.

I feel sorry for his wife; it must be terrible for a girl to marry a man for life, then find out that he hasn't got one.

His cousin Ferdy was the unluckiest pilot in the history of British aviation . . . he lost his life in a simulator crash!

If you want ugliness, stupidity and failure, don't look at me.
But if you want charisma, brains and wealth . . .
I'll get you someone else!

I get no respect; when Special Branch tapped my 'phone, they reversed the charges.

I suppose it runs in the family. I remember my uncle used to say, 'Mitch my boy . . . life is a parade!'
. . . poor old bastard got run over by a float!

I have to consider my dependants – two children, one ex-wife and the Inland Revenue.

Bernie McGill is a man who started his career at the bottom . . . and stayed there!

Bernie is well known for his wardrobe . . . so many men have been found hiding inside it.

He has no luck with women . . . when he 'phoned an 0891 sex line, the girl said, 'Not tonight dear, I've got an earache!'

Unlucky? If he went into the funeral business, people would stop dying!

LOVE

'Oh life is a glorious cycle of song,
A medley of extemporanea;
And love is a thing that can never go wrong
And I am Marie of Romania.'

(Dorothy Parker)

She: Do you love me still?
He: No, I prefer it when you move around a bit.

I'm burning with passion! I want you now!
There's no time to go to bed . . . let's hop into the
microwave!

I met a wonderful girl on the Internet: Dot
Comm.

She was German. Our relationship was purely
Teutonic.

I offered her a ring and she gave me the finger.

I loved her for her mind . . . until I found out that
sex was the furthest thing from it!

I'm happy to announce that next Saturday, Alan and Rita will be celebrating their twentieth marriage counsellor!

Alan's been happily married to Rita for twenty-eight years . . . Rita's been happily married to Alan for . . . two years!

They tell me that a relationship is a lot of work. Well, frankly, the last thing I need is a second job.

'I never married; I didn't like the hours!'
(Angela Colley)

We planned a runaway marriage and, sure enough, three months later, she ran away and got married!

Did I ever tell you about the time I fell in love with a lady decorator? I was overcome with emulsion!

MASONIC

'*The heart which conceals, and the tongue which ne'er reveals.*'

The issue of whether Freemasons have secrets or not, is a closely guarded secret. As I've never been a Mason, all I can do is offer a few lines suitable for use at social functions, hosted by people who do things I wouldn't be allowed to tell you about if I were one of them, but I'm not, so it's all right.

Nurse!

SPEECH EXCERPTS:

Worshipful Master, honoured guests, brethren, ladies and gentlemen:
Before I start, the manager of Hilltops Golf and Country Club has asked me to make a special announcement: those of you who left your cars to be parked by one of the valet parking attendants, please contact Crayborne Police immediately . . . the club doesn't *have* any valet parking attendants!

I've been asked to apologise on behalf of Ray Bearsley. For those of you who don't know, Ray is our treasurer and – to be truthful – any organisation has a right to be nervous when its treasurer suddenly leaves the country.
Nevertheless, Ray has vowed to treat the lodge's money as if it were his own . . . and that makes me even more nervous!

Before he left, Ray worked out the cost of that delicious meal we've just had. He calculated that pound for pound, it would have been cheaper to eat a Lexus!
Still, as long as you enjoyed it, that's the main thing.

I've been given the honour of proposing a toast to the ladies, but I'm sure they won't mind sharing their slice of toast tonight, with our other honoured guests.

Masonry embraces people from all walks of life, and it's only natural that our guests should reflect a similar healthy cross-section. Apart from the family and friends of our membership, we're happy to welcome representatives and observers from some prominent organisations this evening . . .

There are people here from the Confederation of British Industry – the CBI, the Electrician's Union – the EETPU, the Engineering Union – the AEU . . . and the Farm Owners' Association – the EIEIO!

You know, these evenings are always enjoyable and very special. Tonight is the only chance we have as a group to express our appreciation to our ladies for having tolerated yet another year of absent menfolk.
It's a golden opportunity for us to toast their health, happiness and well-being.

Was there ever a more deserving toast?

In a few moments you'll be hearing the Ladies Song, led by Eddie Freeman, and I think I can assure you that tonight, Eddie is going to sing as he's never sung before . . . in tune!

Without in any way wishing to steal his thunder, ladies and gentlemen, I've taken the liberty of writing a couple of extra verses for the song especially for tonight.

Eat your heart out, Noel Gallagher!

'We thank all you ladies in waiting,
You're almost too good to be true
Your charm and your sweet understanding
Ensures our devotion to you.

So when our lodge meetings are over,
We think about those left alone
Some brothers go back to their loved ones
And some of the others . . . go home.'

Gentlemen – a toast to the honey . . . the ladies!

LADY'S REPLY: *See* Round Table, Rotary and Others

MORE EXCERPTS:

You'll be relieved to hear that I don't intend to use the full two hours allotted to me for my speech . . . my position in the Dillon Lodge is relatively junior and I don't want to push my luck!

Apart from that, I'd really like to get through this before the Prozac begins to wear off!

You know, you meet the nicest people in Masonry, and some of the nicest of the nicest are here tonight.

For a start, let's take Melvyn Wheeler . . . and leave him there.

There aren't too many people like our President –
a man who – over the years – not only kept
his figure, but actually did even better . . .
he doubled it!

I originally intended to refer to him as 'a pillar of
the Masonic movement'. Luckily, just in time, I
looked up the word 'pillar' in the dictionary and
it said, 'pillar: something that's thick, immovable
and holds things up'.

. . . so we can't use that!

And yet, merely to call Melvyn 'a Freemason', is
a bit like calling Michelangelo a 'decorator'!

Over the years, he's done such good work that,
frankly, he would have been made Grand Master
by now if there was any justice in this world . . .
luckily there isn't!

For the benefit of our guests, perhaps I should
explain that the gentleman who announced you
when you arrived this evening, is our Director of
Ceremonies, Dick Langham.
As a DC, he goes strictly by the book . . .
unfortunately, the book was written by the
Marquis de Sade!

Another important job in Freemasonry, is that of
almoner. Our almoner is Terry Francis and,
believe me, we're lucky to have him . . . very few
people could do a job like that.
It's really difficult to think of *anyone* else capable
of filling his shoes . . . especially since half the
time he can't remember where he left 'em!

'May Masonry flourish till nature expire
And its glories ne'er fade till the world is on fire.'
(Anon) (with a little help from his wife, Mrs Anon)

(*See also* Round Table, Rotary and Others)

MEAN AND TIGHT-FISTED

We're paying tribute today, to Angus McPherson,
a man known affectionately as 'Old Virgin
Pockets'!

It's not that he's mean, he just doesn't like giving
money away once he's memorised the serial
numbers.

Angus is saving his money for a rainy century!

Angus McPherson has that special talent for
being able to drink on an empty pocket.

But, of course, he *is* handicapped; he's profoundly
hard of spending.

What can you say about a man who goes to the
pictures on standby?!

He's kept his money folded for so long, the Queen has an ingrowing tiara!

It obviously runs in the family . . . his little son's teacher asked him, 'If you had six apples and I asked for one, how many apples would you have left?'
The kid said, 'Six'.

He's a sentimental man and a frugal man . . .
he still has the 'Little Chef' serviettes from his wedding reception.

You know, there must be insanity in his family . . .
they keep writing to him for money.

NAUGHTY BOYS

'Early to bed, early to rise,
I wish my willie was a bigger size.'
                    (Too embarrassed to attribute.)

Duncan Bradley started going out with girls fairly late in life . . . about two years into his marriage!

I've no idea what to get him for his birthday . . .
I mean, what do you get for the man who's had everybody?

He's quite a guy; only twenty-five and he's already had seven wives . . . three of his own and four of his friends'.

He keeps forgetting things . . . like the fact that he's married!

I don't know how many affairs he's had but I wish I had the catering contract.

He's had so much on the side, he walks with a limp.

He celebrated his silver wedding with a romantic dinner for two at the Waterside Inn . . .
His wife just stayed in and watched TV.

Every woman looks alike to him . . . worth one.

Truth is stranger than fiction . . . but when you come home at 3am, and your wife wants to know where you've been, you'd better go for fiction!

(*See also* Two-Timers)

NAUGHTY GIRLS

'If all those sweet young things were laid end to end, I wouldn't be a bit surprised!'

(Dorothy Parker)

This is the woman who started going for grief counselling the day her local shop ran out of Duracell batteries.

Last year, when she went to Rome, she saw more ceilings than Michelangelo.

She was a circus performer – a high wire artiste – and her husband caught her in the act!

I always wondered why she kept a visitors book on her bedside table!

She'd make a lousy cattle woman; she can't keep her calves together!

They used to teach the birds and the bees about *her*.

She *had* to do it on the first date . . . she never got a second one.

For a girl who was studying law, she didn't put up much of a defence.

She was always talking about wanting to have a catered affair, and then one day her husband found her in bed with the delicatessen man!

He was livid when he caught her at it. 'After all I've done for you!' he cried, 'I've bought you a lovely home, a beautiful car, a diamond necklace . . . and you could at least stop while I'm talking to you'!

She said she's had two improper suggestions made to her tonight, and she's very offended . . . normally she gets at least a dozen!

(*See also* Two-Timers)

OPENERS

Good evening. My name is Greg Patterson. I'm here to help you through your after-dinner nap.

Please excuse me if I seem a little edgy this evening. I had to stand all the way from Kings Cross to Hammersmith . . . and that's not easy in a mini cab!

They say you should only speak in public for the same length of time you can make love in private . . . so I'd like to wind up by saying . . .

I've been chosen to be your Master of Ceremonies tonight and quite frankly, at this stage, there's not an awful lot you can do about that.

Before I start, I'd like to thank all the previous speakers for whipping this audience into a frenzy of enthusiasm.

Isn't this exciting? Everybody who's nobody is here tonight.

I hope you can all hear me at the back . . . because the people in the *front* certainly don't want to know!

(When you're hosting a small party):

The first thing I'd like to say this evening is, I'm afraid I left all my credit cards at home so . . . anybody got any cash?

'I'm delighted tonight, to be surrounded by so many good friends. The last time I had a feeling as warm as this, I found I'd wet myself!'

(Gwyn Headley)

As I look around the room this evening, and see so many intelligent faces looking up at me with sharp anticipation, I think of the speech I'm about to make, and I suddenly realise . . . Bloody Hell! I'm in big trouble!

Family and friends . . . I say 'family and friends' because I feel I know too much about you to call you ladies and gentlemen . . .

Thank you for that wonderful sitting ovation.

I think I should begin by explaining that, on occasions like this, the length of the speech I make is based on a formula which is scaled according to the fee I'm paid; the higher the fee, the longer the speech.
So thank you all very much . . . goodnight.

Thank you for keeping the applause nice and short . . . as you know, despite the hours I spend practising my modesty, I find it very difficult to look humble for any length of time, so I do appreciate your co-operation.

Well, it's always great to be among friends . . . pity none of them turned up tonight, really.

I must confess, until yesterday, I wasn't really sure
what I was going to talk about this evening . . .
I suppose I could have waffled on about nothing
very much until it was time for me to sit down
and have a brandy, but frankly, I didn't want
mine to be like all the other speeches I've heard in
previous years . . .

These days, people are so tense and stressed out,
that they seem to have a lot of trouble falling
asleep. Well, ladies and gentlemen, if the last
speech I made is anything to go by, I think I may
be able to help.

I've been asked to say a few words today, because
the staff want to get home early and they figured
that if I made a speech it would be the quickest
way to clear the room.

Now I'm not going to stand up here tonight and
bore you with a load of corny old jokes; we've
got plenty of speakers still to come this evening
who'll take care of all that . . .

I must say, it's always a pleasure to be in the
company of civilised, decent, intelligent people . . .
But of course, I also enjoy evenings like these.

(*See* more openers in other sections)

QUIPS AND BITS

Here are a few random comments and some remedies for potentially embarrassing situations.

Firstly, have any of you heard me speak before?
Well, it's the same old crap again, I'm afraid.

Thank you . . . kindly be seated . . .
Please! Only one chair per person!

I don't have to be here at all, you know; I could have 'phoned the speech in!

Lowering microphone . . .

If I'd listened to my mother and stood up straight, I wouldn't have to do this!

Some of you at the back might not be able to hear me . . . so I think it's only fair that I give you guys in the front, a chance to go back and join them.

Writing jokes is easy . . . all you have to do is laugh, then think backwards.

You know, some of these gags are so old, they shouldn't be up this late!

I've got bad news for you . . . that was my best joke!

After a slip-up . . .

If you think that was a mistake, you should have seen my first wife!

That's the first time this ever happened again!

Small turnout . . .

Did you all come in the same car?

As we have such a small turnout tonight, I'd really appreciate it if you could all applaud twice as loud when I finish.

. . . And so I ask you all . . . do we really need rhetorical questions?

One thing's for certain . . . nobody knows for sure!

I hereby declare the motion curried . . . er . . . carried!

If someone starts leaving during your speech . . .

> **If you're going for a pizza, I'll have anchovies, mozzarella and tomato.**

> **Don't tell me, let me guess . . . you're so impressed by my speech you're going out to tell your friends, right?**

> **Okay, Okay . . . a little boredom never hurt anyone!**

> **Don't blame me, I stole these jokes from Frank Skinner.**

> **Thank you ladies and gentlemen for sharing this death scene with me.**

Cold room . . .

> **Ladies and gentlemen, I'd like to announce that the room this evening, is sponsored by Zanussi Refrigeration.**

(*See also* Hecklers, Waffle)

RETIREMENT

There are two kinds of retirees – them what wanna go and them what don't.

Either way, it can be a traumatic time, and the occasion should be handled with sensitivity.

Ernest Hemingway described retirement as 'the ugliest word in the language'. As if to reinforce his attitude, Ernie blew his brains out at the age of sixty-two.

If you sense that your colleague or friend dreads retirement, and sees it only as signing on for God's waiting list, try to concentrate on the positive aspects of what should be a new phase in his or her life.

After all, there'll be more free time to devote to hobbies and interests – possibly to begin a brand new project; many people starting out well past the age of sixty, have created fabulously successful enterprises.

For the younger man, say in his fifties, the distinction between early retirement and redundancy may appear merely academic, and can so easily damage that vital sense of self-esteem. Boost his ego, admire his skill and experience, tell him how much he'll be missed – even if you hate the bastard.

On the other hand, the person leaving may feel totally fulfilled at the culmination of a long and happy career. You can then afford to be a little more abrasive with your humour.

Be aware of all these possibilities as you select your one-liners.

He looks forward to the golden years ahead, with
the optimism of a truly spiritual and religious
man. Every day he gets on his knees and prays
. . . he prays he can get *off* his knees!

Retirement is the time of life when you can stop
lying about your age and start lying about the
house.

Sixty-five. That's the age when you've acquired
enough experience to lose your job.

'Retirement at sixty-five is ridiculous! When I was
sixty-five, I still had pimples!'
(George Burns 1896-1996)

TOAST: Here's to the holidays. Bless all three
hundred and sixty-five of them.

Stuart, when we heard you were about to retire,
we passed round the hat to buy you a gift. Not
only didn't we raise any money . . . but somebody
nicked the bloody hat!

The problem with being retired is that your week
lacks any shape.
It has no real form . . . no misery of Monday
mornings, no relief of Friday afternoons, no
difference on the weekends . . .

You never know what day it is, what time it is,
where you're supposed to be . . .
Come to think of it, it'll be exactly like you were
still working here.

A few lines for your own retirement . . .

You have no idea, ladies and gentlemen, how
wonderful it feels, knowing that forty-five busy
people have turned up here this evening just to
see me quit.

. . . still, you know what they say, 'Give the
public what they want'.

As you can imagine, for quite some time I've been
anticipating my retirement and making plans for
the next step, and for the years ahead.

The other day I decided to review my situation. I
gained access to my retirement fund . . . shook it
. . . unscrewed the lid and emptied it out.

Pathetic, isn't it?

Perhaps now you'll understand the depth of my
gratitude . . . not only for twenty-six happy years
at Blake's, but also for the free dinner this
evening.

It *was* free, wasn't it?

Tonight has been a very pleasant way to round
off a most rewarding career . . .

I'm really grateful to all those who organised it and to everybody who came along to share this very special evening with me.

Thank you all.

(*See also* Age)

REUNIONS

Ladies and gentlemen . . .
Since June 1972, you survived . . .
One year, eight months of Edward Heath,
Two years of Harold Wilson,
Three years of James Callaghan,
Eleven and a half years of Margaret Thatcher,
Six years, six months of John Major . . .
and seven months of Tony Blair . . .
so I'm sure you'll be able to put up with ten minutes of me!

I must say it's very nice to look around the room tonight and see so many old friends, and a few new faces . . . and frankly, some of the old friends could *do* with new faces.

If last year's dinner is anything to go by, I think we should let this one go by as well!

You know, a lot has happened to all of us since
we were pupils here at Baldwin Grammar School
– some of us became lawyers, accountants,
politicians, stockbrokers . . . others became *useful*
members of society!

Happiness is going to a school reunion and
learning that the kid who was voted most likely
to succeed . . . didn't.

Isn't it fun to get together and see who's falling
apart?

Twenty years ago, when inflation in Britain was
at its height, it was announced that a bird in the
hand was worth *three* in the bush! . . .
When you passed 'Go', you collected £285 . . .
and to make sure you satisfied your lover . . .
*five*play!

Some of the guys I was at school with got so fat
and bald they didn't even recognise me.

Those were the decadent days of debauchery;
people we knew used to swap wives and sniff
cocaine . . . or was it the other way around?

RICH AND POOR

'*When I was young, I used to think that wealth and power would bring me happiness . . . I was right.*'
(Gahan Wilson – Cartoonist)

Tony enjoys the good life . . . he's not allowed to enjoy the bad life. Anne won't let him.

You owe it to yourself to be a success . . . from then on, you owe it to the Inland Revenue!

He came from a very wealthy family but he had a lot of pride. One day, he decided he wanted to do something all on his own, so he went and had a wee-wee!

He lives in a very exclusive area – it's so discreet even the Police are ex-directory!

The Neighbourhood Watch is a Rolex.

He's the proud owner of the world's first satellite dishwasher!

Money is not a problem, especially where his health is concerned. He's hired Carl Fogarty to come over every morning and kick-start his pacemaker.

Tony has a lovely farm . . . it's a prosperous and humane farm.
He's made sure that every pig has its own pen . . . a Parker 51!

His yacht was so big, you had to start out for the rail on a Monday if you were going to throw up on a Friday!

He takes his urine samples to the doctor in a crystal decanter!

He gets his children from Harrods.

He loves his little luxuries . . . he's even got his own jet!
. . . only on his gas cooker, but it's a start.

Last week he went out to buy a couple of golf clubs . . . Wentworth and St. Andrew's!

Recently, he cashed a cheque that was so big . . . the bank bounced!

There are three taps on his bathroom basin:
'Hot', 'Cold' and 'Dom Perignon'!

The two great tests of character are wealth and poverty.

He was up against the wall so often, the writing was on him!

'Mere wealth can't bring me happiness
Mere wealth can't make me glad
But I'm quite willing to take a shot
At being rich and sad.'   (Anon)

Blaming poverty on the wealthy, makes as much sense as blaming sickness on the healthy.

There's only one thing stopping me from being rich . . . I haven't got any money!

Money can't buy happiness . . . certainly not the money *I* get!

At one time, I went five days without food or drink . . . finally, the waiter came.

ROASTS AND INSULTS

Choose your customers carefully when using these rude lines. Remember, some people are sensitive to criticism. Especially the fat, ugly, stupid ones!

I've just heard that Pete Martin has been given a great honour in his home town of Wigan.
They've named a street after him! The mayor was quoted as saying, 'I know that pride will fill the hearts of the people of Wigan as they walk along Prick Street . . .'

A man like Pete Martin comes along just once in a lifetime.
Isn't it a pity he had to come along in *our* lifetime?!

Here's the good news: it's been said that what he lacks in size, he makes up for in quickness.
Here's the bad news: it was his wife who said it!

As for his hidden talents . . . well, the search goes on.

Words cannot express my feelings for this man . . . *fingers* can!
(Make the gesture)

His talent is beyond dispute . . . everybody agrees he has none!

But he's a nice guy deep down and sometimes that's where I wish he was!

He's more than a friend . . . he's a total stranger!

Nobody thinks more highly of him than I do and that means he's got a problem 'cos I think he's a prat!

And I say this all to his *face* . . . because I'd look silly talking to his arse!

I'm one of his old friends . . . he can't *get* new ones!

His ambition is to be filthy rich . . . well, so far, he's halfway there . . .

If there's such a thing as reincarnation, he's coming back as a human being.

Phil was a premature baby . . . he was born three months before his parents had a chance to get married!

Some people bring happiness wherever they go.
Pete Martin brings happiness *when*ever he goes.

But I can identify with this guy. After all, I'm a
bit of a prick myself.

When he was a kid, like other youngsters, he used
to play 'Hide and Seek'.
Trouble was, when he was hiding, nobody
noticed the difference.

His personality defeats even Fujicolor.

This man has always reminded me of St. Stephen
. . . St. Stephen is a small, dull town in Wales.

Don't worry, this'll do him good – exposing these
faults is just my way of making a small
contribution to his humility.

'Cedric' was his given name . . . he was too
young to refuse it.

ROUND TABLE, ROTARY AND OTHERS

'*Fellowship: A make-believe compact for purposes of piffle.*'
(Elbert Hubbard)

ROUND TABLE

(All lines are interchangeable or adaptable, and will work for most clubs and associations.)

Stan Pearce is responsible for our big membership drive. He's driven out eight members already.

Stan is the guy who writes the table plans around here, so I think I'd better stop making jokes about him, or next year I'll find myself sitting in the car park!

I must admit, I wasn't quite sure what to talk about today.
I considered telling you about a recent conversation I had with the chairman during which he gave me intimate details of a certain lady who's had passionate affairs with at least three members of the committee, but then I thought . . . 'Naaah . . . you wouldn't be interested in all that!'

I'm delighted to see such a good turnout this evening; you obviously didn't know I was going to be making a speech . . .

Andrew Scott is area chairman of Round Table, and as such is responsible for twenty tables in this district.
Scotty has everything it takes to be a success . . . a quiet charm, a persuasive manner, the ability to grovel without wrinkling his suit . . .

LINES FOR A LADY REPLYING TO A TOAST

Years ago, in the days when it was considered unseemly for a lady to speak in public, the response to a toast would have been made – on her behalf – by a bachelor. Thankfully, we've come a long way since then.

Firstly, may I say that to have been asked to reply on behalf of the ladies this evening, is a very great honour . . . and absolutely terrifying!

I think my husband Ian realised just how nervous I was a few minutes ago, when he asked the wine waiter to recommend something that goes well with finger-nails!

Thank you, Trevor, for those words of flattery . . . I think I have some idea now, of how a pancake feels when they pour syrup on it.

As a long-time Round Table widow, I'm going to start with a few words of comfort for any of the newer ladies who may feel insecure from time to time when their menfolk are out late or away on Round Table jaunts.

My advice is: don't worry. I once had a little dog who used to chase cars, and believe me, even if by chance he'd ever caught one, he wouldn't have known what to do with it!

The essential thing to remember is the ongoing benefit produced as a result of all those fun and games.

As long as the members of Fensbury Round Table find fulfilment and enjoyment in the pursuit of their various activities, countless local charities and causes will continue to profit as a result, and that's good enough for me.

Contented husbands and an enriched community . . . those are the reasons I'm happy to continue giving my support.

On behalf of the ladies, I wish you all continued success.

Long may the good work continue.

Thank you, Fensbury, for your hospitality this evening . . . you've made us all feel very much at home.

ROTARY

Mr President, Mr District Governor, distinguished guests, fellow Rotarians, waiters and waitresses, ladies and gentlemen:

I think that covers everyone.

May I begin by assuring you that I *am* fully aware of the grave responsibility I have, as a featured speaker on Charter Night, to all the members and to our guests on such a special occasion . . .

I decided some time ago, to make the effort, to prepare well in advance, and to speak this evening, as I've never spoken before . . . coherently!

It's my pleasure, on behalf of my fellow members, to welcome our many visiting Rotarians . . .

For your benefit, gentlemen, especially if this is your first visit, I'd like to point out that we're very fortunate in our branch; we're rich with characters . . .

we have all types here . . .

the dignified, the restrained, the sensitive, the intelligent . . . and . . . the majority.

Gentlemen – Napoleon said, 'Glory is fleeting, but obscurity is forever!'
It's a pity he never met our honoured treasurer, Leo Poulson . . .

For those of our guests who may find themselves in conversation with Leo a little later, I'm confident you'll find there won't be a dull moment . . . trust me . . . it'll last all the way through!

But when it comes to a Rotary Club treasurer, who needs excitement?

After all, as active fund-raisers, surely, we're safer with our money in the hands of a solid, steady, competent official . . .

A mild-mannered quiet man . . .

You know . . . like Crippen.

A man with that magic ability to light up a room . . . as soon as he *leaves* it.

By the way, this evening Leo has brought with him two old members . . . one at his table, the other one – in his trousers!

Welcome, all of you.

LINES FOR A ROTARY PRESIDENT

. . . To be serious for thirty-six seconds, I suppose the main feature of my year is that I've tried to shift the emphasis of our charitable endeavours so that the benefits favour our own community to a greater extent than before.

Although I would never underestimate the crucial national and international role Rotarians continue to play, I believe that if more Rotary

Clubs concentrated on charity beginning at home, a lot more money could be raised world-wide.

Local support is vital to the success of any function. Surely that support will be greater and more enthusiastic if people see the fruits of our charitable work having an effect right there in their own community.

With this very much in mind, we were able to raise over £9,000 as a result of our special cocktail evenings . . .
We had some interesting visiting speakers . . . a body language expert who could tell your sexual preferences and degree of satisfaction from your handwriting!

I suppose it depended on how shaky it was . . .

A spiritualist who claimed to communicate with the dear departed and was able to tell if you were having an affair, just by holding an item of clothing . . . your girlfriend's bra!

And a talented wine connoisseur who could work out from just one sip of wine, not only the year it was produced, not only the vineyard, but also the name and address of the guy who jumped on the bloody grapes!

As I come to the end of my year, I have – quite naturally – mixed feelings.
To a fellow like me, hard work is second nature. *First* nature is . . . buggering about!

. . . and with this job, I haven't been able to do that.

But I have had some wonderful support from those characters I was insulting earlier . . . it's been a real pleasure to work alongside the committee, the sub-committees and the members of this Rotary Club, and it's nice to have an opportunity, publicly, to say so.

Honoured guests . . . please remain seated whilst the members of Tile Kiln Rotary Club drag themselves to an upright position and raise their glasses to you. But don't be *too* flattered . . . these buggers will drink to anything!
Gentlemen . . . our guests and visitors!

TOAST: As we meet on the level, may we part on the square.

(*See also* Masonic)

SEX AND SEXISM

Get ready Salman, after these gags I may have to move in with you.

Urgh!

I won't be speaking for too long, my girlfriend's waiting for me. We're playing 'Sink the Titanic' tonight, and she's the North Atlantic!

How I yearn to whisper sweet nothings into her lap!

It's difficult to believe, I know, but I've actually been celibate now for many, many hours.

Changing girlfriends has done me the world of good . . . I feel a different woman!

I tend to place women upon a pedestal . . . then I like to push 'em in and flush 'em away!

I never went in for one-night stands . . . I couldn't put up with a woman for that length of time!

I'll believe women are truly equal the day I see one with 'Dad' tattooed on her chest.

I've always been highly sexed . . . at my school's sport's day in 1978, I won the three-legged race all by myself.

You can't judge a man's horsepower by the size of his exhaust.

There's a theory as to why women have orgasms . . . it's just something else to moan about!

She: You men are animals! You'll jump on anything that moves!
He: Don't be ridiculous. They don't have to move!

When it came to love-making, she was hoping he'd be a slow-cooker . . . as it turned out, what she got was a microwave!

Someone told him the most important thing in sex is foreplay . . . so he invited another couple.

I don't know what his performance was like on their wedding night . . . all I *do* know is that on the outside of their hotel bedroom door, Shirley left a notice saying: 'Disturb'!

His last girlfriend had a beautiful face, a superb figure, and only took fourteen minutes to inflate!

One day, she fell out with him, but he managed to patch things up!

Nowadays, he leads a pretty lonely life . . . poor bastard stays in every night playing strip patience!

SHORTIES

'Being short never bothered me for three seconds . . . the rest of the time I wanted to commit suicide!'
(Mel Brooks)

This man would be six feet tall if they ever straightened out his legs.

He's not long for this world; he's only five foot four.

All his ancestors were short . . . his family tree is a stump!

When he worked on a farm, he used to milk the cows standing up.

He's very superstitious . . . he believes it's unlucky to walk under a black cat.

He'll never need to go to a shrink . . . he's already shrunk.

SHOWS

What a star-studded night! Pavarotti sang, Bob Monkhouse told jokes, Wayne Sleep danced and Antony Hopkins strangled a waiter and ate his liver!

They gave me a seat right up in the 'gods' . . . I've never been so high up before . . .

I said to the guy next to me, 'How do you like the show?'
He said, 'What show? I'm flying the shuttle to Glasgow!'

Half way through the show, people were yelling 'More! More! More!' . . . They were calling for Maurice Moore – he's the guy whose job it was to pull down the curtain.

The show was so bad, the audience booed the ice cream girl!

All the audience was booing except for one man, he was applauding . . . he was applauding the people who were booing.

SPIVS

'He who sells what isn't his'n,
Must buy it back, or go to prison.'

(Daniel Drew)

A little later on this evening, we're going to hold a free draw; first prize is £50 . . . second prize is Harry Fisher's cheque for £300!

Harry *seems* too good to be true . . . he isn't.

He's a man of convictions . . . admittedly, most of them were overturned on appeal!

But he's genuine. He's as genuine as a hooker's orgasm!

Recently, he formed himself into a Limited Credibility Company.

Harry suffers from truth decay.

Even his *cash* bounces!

He's a man who believes that honesty is the best poverty.

In our community, this man is an icon.
Icon!
In fact, that's his motto.

He used to be in pictures . . . with little serial numbers across the bottom.

He was always a fine figure of a man . . . tall, dark and handcuffed.

Back in the eighties, he spent a year in a tax-shelter . . .
Ford *Open* tax shelter.

Of course, he was only following in his father's fingerprints.

But he's a sentimental old softie really.
He's still got the first fiver he ever embezzled.

SPORT

Drug sampling takes up so much time now at Olympic events that the organisers are thinking of introducing a new event . . . 'Synchronised Urinating'.

He's a great athlete, but he's not too smart. At the Tokyo Olympics he won a Gold Medal . . . he wanted to cherish it forever, so he had it bronzed!

If exercise is so damned healthy, why do so many athletes have to retire at thirty-five?!

He can ski for hours on end . . . in fact, that's his normal position.

He's too unco-ordinated to be any good at skiing
. . . last year, he went to St. Moritz and he broke
two pairs of skis, fell down in the snow six times,
ran over two old ladies, sprained his arm and
slammed into a tree . . . and that was just getting
out of the car!

I suppose snooker's all right, but quite frankly I
prefer sex . . .
it's much more fun and you don't have to put
chalk on the end of your stick!

One of my girlfriends is a tennis player . . . to her,
love means nothing!

She has a service no one can return . . . it always
hits the net first!

I told her I was a little stiff from rugby.
She said, 'It doesn't matter where you come from,
it's what's inside your heart that matters.'

Rugby is a great way to meet new people:
ambulance drivers, nurses, paramedics,
orthopaedic surgeons . . .

He's mad about animals; dogs, horses, cats,
hamsters . . . he doesn't care *what* he shoots!

Those of us who are really close to him realise that
Noel is a great guy, a staunch friend and – in all
aspects of his life – absolutely straight as a die . . .
which is a bloody sight more than you can say for
his *shooting*!

Apparently, after they saw the standard of
accuracy this afternoon, a gang of real live
pigeons have now decided that, for them, this
club is one of the safest places in the county.
Realising that most of the shooters here are a
danger only to themselves, the pigeons have
actually come up with a new sport of their own
for next year's meeting . . . it's called, 'Surfing
the Clay'.

TOAST
Here's to our fisherman bold,
Here's to the fish he caught,
Here's to the one that got away
And here's to the one he bought!

Many a man nurses a secret ambition: to
outsmart horses, fish and women.

He described the one that got away by using a
finger and a thumb . . . he was a shrimp boat
captain!

And now let's hear it for the fish . . .

'Enjoy thy stream, O harmless fish,
And when an angler for his dish
Through gluttony's vile sin
Attempts, the wretch, to pull thee out,
God give thee strength, O gentle trout,
To pull the rascal in.'

I had a great day at the races last Monday . . .
I didn't go!

Recently, I've been suffering from my old sports
injury – 'racecourse pocket'.

I nearly won a bundle on the Grand National last
year; my horse was right up there alongside the
winning horse . . . then the race started!

I should have realised it wasn't much of a horse.
For a start, he was hung like a man!

Nigel supports Brighton and Hove Albion . . .
and that says it all really, doesn't it?
Well, his doctor *did* tell him to avoid any
excitement.

That team is very similar to an old fashioned bra
. . . no cups and poor support!

Last Saturday, their goalie missed such an easy save that in despair, he put his head in his hands . . . and missed that too!

Footballers are such wimps . . . yesterday, one player was injured during the coin-toss!

You know what the trouble is with referees? They don't give a shit who wins!

Toxteth is as bad as ever . . . I was up there last week, watching a load of hooligans fighting in the streets, and before I knew it, a football match broke out!

You know, it's fascinating watching international cricket on Sky Sports.
A recent statistical analysis revealed that cricket players spend one per cent of their time hitting, four per cent of their time catching and ninety-five per cent of their time scratching.

Next season, England is going to be playing the West Indies at Lourdes . . . let's face it, they'll *need* a bloody miracle!

Everyone knows it's a healthy life in Australia. While I was in Sydney, I tried skin-diving, pot-holing and bare-back riding . . . and that was just in my hotel bedroom!

STUPID

They say that blood is thicker than water . . .
Charlie Rowland is thicker than both!

When he was circumcised, they threw the wrong
bit away!

Believe it or not, Charlie was very advanced at
school . . . all the other kids in his class were
eight years old, Charlie was fourteen!

It's fair to say he wasn't in the top half of his
class, but he *was* in the half that made the top
half possible.

Talk about thick! Once, during a power cut at
Leicester Square Station, he was stuck on an
escalator for four hours!
I asked him, 'Why didn't you just walk down?' . . .
He said, 'I was on my way *up*!'

Someone told him ninety per cent of all accidents
happen in the home, so he moved.

No, he's not very bright. One day when his wife
said, 'Do me a favour, change the baby', he came
home with a different kid!

One thing's for sure . . . no one will ever try to bump him off because he knows too much!

He's a man of few words . . . and even fewer thoughts.

He's at his wit's end. It was a very short journey.

He's several Air Miles short of a trip to Paris; one time he stole a car and kept up the payments.

Charlie may talk like an idiot, and act like an idiot, but don't let that fool you . . . he *is* an idiot!

I'll never forget the secretary we had in our Dublin office; every time the little bell sounded on her typewriter, she broke for tea.

Sometimes I think she had her ears pierced too deep.

Tracey knows nothing about sewing . . . she thinks a thimble is a thort of thign!

She's no better in the kitchen; she tried to bake a cake recently and the recipe said, 'Separate two eggs' . . . so she put one in the living room and one in the hall!

My wife's always complaining about toys lying around the house. The worrying thing is, we don't have any children!

No true Irishman would ever allow himself to be buried in anything but an Irish grave . . . he'd rather die first!

According to the last census, Liverpool has the densest population . . . it also has the most people per mile!

SURPRISE PARTIES

Every now and then, well-meaning friends decide to spring a so-called 'surprise' party on a so-called 'unsuspecting' honouree.

In my experience, very few of these celebrations genuinely surprise the victim. Somewhere along the line, someone is bound to have tipped them off – either deliberately or through simply being careless – and the poor 'springee' has to play along with the whole charade and pretend to be gobsmacked.

If you have a special birthday or other milestone coming up, and people are acting just a little too casually, it's as well to have an 'impromptu' speech handy.

During the evening, pretend to be making notes, so that people will believe that you threw a couple of words together on the spot.

In order to sound convincing, the lines you use should be very brief and not too clever.

Well done. You've come to the right place for not too clever.

You know, when I first saw you all this evening, and suddenly realised I'd been had, I thought, 'How wonderful . . . all the people I really care about have turned up just to celebrate my birthday . . .'

Of course, once I was over the shock, I remembered that it's not just any birthday, it's my *sixtieth* . . . so now I'm not really sure whether you're here to celebrate, or to *gloat*.

Incidentally, I think you should know that a surprise like this can be a little dangerous at my age . . . you were taking quite a risk.

Nevertheless, you've made tonight a very special night for me and I'd like to thank each and every one of you for paying me such a great compliment and for organising this piss uh . . . I mean this little party.

I must tell you, until this evening, I never realised how well my darling wife Jean could keep a secret, and that's bloody worrying . . .

God knows what *else* she's been keeping quiet about!

Thank you, Cyril, for your very kind words. I know you don't usually *do* sincerity, so it really was praise indeed.

You know, they say that if you don't care how old you are, you're young . . .
if you *lie* about how old you are, you're middle aged . . .
and if you *boast* about how old you are, let's face it, you're old!

Well, I'm not really sure which category I'm in, but I must tell you that I rather *like* being called a 'sexagenarian' . . . at this time of life it sounds like flattery.

Of course, sixty on the calendar is a bit like sixty on the road . . . everybody seems to be overtaking you . . .

But it does have it's compensations . . .

As Maurice Chevalier said, 'I'm glad I'm not young anymore.'

. . . Hey . . . I wonder how he feels about being dead!

Thank you so much for this wonderful surprise, and for all the work you've put into making tonight's party so enjoyable . . .
I really couldn't imagine a happier way of celebrating anything. Believe me, no man could ask for a better birthday present than the one you've all given me by coming here this evening.

Good luck, God bless and good health to you all.

Thanks for everything.

(*See also* Birthdays)

TOASTS

APRIL FOOLS' DAY
'Let us toast the fools.
But for them, the rest of us could not succeed.'
(Mark Twain)

CATERING
'We may live without poetry, music and art,
We may live without conscience and live without heart,
We may live without friends, we may live without books.
But civilised man cannot live without cooks.'
(Owen Meredith)

FRIENDSHIP
Here's champagne to our real friends,
And real pain to our sham friends.

To best friends, who know the worst about us
but refuse to believe it.

'Here's to us that are here,
To you that are there
And the rest of everyone everywhere.'
(Rudyard Kipling)

GENERAL

You treat me like dirt, so here's mud in your eye.

Here's to happy days . . . any twit can have a good time at night!

Here's to you, here's to me
May we never disagree.
But if we do, to hell with you
And here's to me!

A 'GROAST'

(That's a combination of Grace and a toast.)

Bless this bunch while they munch lunch.

HEALTH

I drink to your health when I'm with you
I drink to your health when alone
I drink to your health so often
I've just about buggered my own!

HOSTESS

Here's to the hostess who has worried all day,
And trembled lest everything go the wrong way;
May the grace of contentment possess her at once,
May her guests and her husband do all the right stunts.

(With apologies to Francis Wilson, who wrote 'servants', not 'husband'.)

HUSBANDS

To our husbands . . . men when they are boys,
Boys when they are men; and lovable always!

INTERNATIONAL

Arabic:	'Besalamati!' (Peace), 'Bismillah', 'Fi schettak'.
Belgian:	'Op Uw Gezonheid!' (To your health)
Chinese:	'Kan bei!', 'Wen lie', 'Nien Nien nu e'.
Danish:	'Skal'
Dutch:	'Proost!'
Finnish:	'Kippis'
French:	'À votre santé!' (To your health)
German:	'Prosit!'
Greek:	'Iss Igian!'
Irish Gaelic:	'Slainte!' (To your health)
Hindi:	'Aanand', 'Jaikind'
Hebrew:	'L' Chayim' (To life)
Italian:	'Cin cin', 'Salute'
Japanese:	'Kampai!', 'Banzai!'
Maori:	'Kia-Ora'
Norwegian:	'Skal'
Polish:	'Na zdrowie!' (To your health)
Portuguese:	'A sua saúde!' (Singular), 'Saude!' (To a group)
Russian:	'Na zdorovia'
Spanish:	'Salud' (Health)
Swedish:	'Skal'
Urdu:	'Sanda Bashi'
Welsh:	'Icchyd da'
Zulu:	'Oogy wawa!'

LADIES

Here's to powder and lipstick,
Here's to mascara and curls,
Here's to sun tan and swim suits;
In other words – here's to the girls!

'To Earth's noblest thing – a woman perfected!'

(James Russell Lowell)

LONG LIFE

Here's hoping you live forever . . .
And that mine is the last voice you hear.

LOYAL TOAST

When proposing this toast, it is not customary to say any more than, 'Her Majesty, the Queen'. Once the loyal toast has been made, the chairman or toastmaster usually gives the OK for smokers to light up.

Here's a suggestion for something a little different at that point.

In the words of the essayist, Robert Burton, who lived from 1577 to 1640, 'Tobacco, divine, rare, superexcellent tobacco, which goes far beyond all other panaceas, potable gold, and philosophers' stones, a sovereign remedy to all diseases' . . .
Ladies and gentlemen, you may now smoke!

Please note that Robert Burton snuffed it at sixty-three years old. Quite a respectable age for an Elizabethan puffer, but – of course– in those days, they hadn't yet been told that smoking killed you at fifty.

MOTHER

To Mother. May she live long enough to forget what little devils we used to be.

ROWING TEAM

Bottoms up!
(Well, maybe not)

SISTER

We've toasted the mother and daughter,
We've toasted the sweetheart and wife,
But somehow we missed her,
Our dear little sister –
The joy of another man's life.

(Use 'wonderful' instead of 'dear little' if your sister is older or a big broad.)

TAX COLLECTORS

To the Inland Revenue . . . you've really got to hand it to them.

TOASTMASTER

We all shall bless our toastmaster,
Wherever he may roam,
If he'll only cut the speeches short
And let us all go home!

WEATHER

To warm words on a cold day.

(*See* individual categories for many more toasts.)

TRIBUTES

Here are some usable examples of 'positive' humour – lines designed to show your respect for the subject of your speech, without being too sycophantic.

When paying tribute to an admired family member, business associate or honoured guest, you really need to break up the monotony of continuous praise.

These little guys are effective 'softeners' and may be inserted into your text exactly as written, or adapted to the world of sport, politics, industry, voluntary work or family life.

The lines are all here. Choose them and use them.
Take the trouble. It's worth it.
Hopefully, your speech will be received and remembered – not merely as lip-service – but as a warm and genuine tribute of admiration and respect.

He's the kind of bloke who goes into a revolving door behind you and comes out first.

I don't want to over-emphasise my admiration for this man, but I have to tell you, I worship the water he walks on.
Sorry, but there it is!

This is a man who has so many letters after his name, he could fill up a bowl of alphabet soup!

Cool? If he were any cooler, he'd be a danger to shipping.

He's a natural philosopher . . . even when he was a little baby, his first words were, 'I wet, therefore I am!'
Well, we're honouring Bill tonight, therefore I'm pleased . . . and I'm equally pleased to see so many of his friends and colleagues all gathered for this tribute.

Bill has been described as the most knowledge-able, respected and influential in his field . . . and who am I to disagree with his mother?

This is how clever he is – he translated the 'Anthology of Civilisation' by Schtuphaussen from the original German. Unfortunately, he translated it into Turkish!
Sometimes you can be *too* bloody clever!

Bill Huntley is a man who's always believed that honesty is the best policy and that money isn't everything.
Mind you, he's been wrong about a few other things as well!

It was in the USA I happened to witness for myself, the esteem in which Bill Huntley is held . . . When he came into the room, everyone got down on their knees.
What an ovation, what an honour . . . what a crap game!

He was always a bon viveur . . . in fact, he was a gourmet toddler! When he sucked his thumb, he used to insist on dipping it in a bechamel sauce with parmesan.

But Bill has my sympathy. I know exactly how he feels. You can't imagine how frustrating it is, being a genius in a world full of bloody idiots.

He used to walk around the park with an old mac round his head, exposing his brains to passing women . . . he was known as 'The Thinking Woman's Flasher'.

But we're lucky to have him in the association . . . he's brilliant!
He has an IQ higher than Ian Paisley's blood pressure.

A lot of people are surprised that Bill is a friend of Cabinet Ministers, top entertainers, royalty . . . but why not? Even *they* need someone to look up to.

As far as anyone can tell, he hasn't got a single redeeming vice.

Finally Bill, as Dorothy Parker said to a friend who had just given birth, 'Congratulations. We all knew you had it in you!'

(*See also* Birthdays)

TWO-TIMERS AND OTHER SINNERS

Excerpt from Mitch Murray's 'Ten Commandments *Lite*':

Thou shalt not scream the name of the Lord in vain
Thou shalt not bear false wetness
Thou shalt not admit adultery
Thou shalt not squeal
Thou shalt not covet thy neighbour's ox, nor his
wife's ass.

PLUS FIVE OTHER EXCITING 'SHALT-NOTS', COM-
ING SOON, TO A DIVORCE COURT NEAR YOU!

He's discovered the secret of sustaining a happy
and satisfying relationship . . . he fools around!

Not all wives are suspicious . . . some of them
know!

She was so concerned with his happiness that she
hired a private detective to find out the cause of it.

One day he started to suspect that she'd been
having headaches with another man!

She was only ever unfaithful to him once . . . with
Real Madrid!

I was engaged to a dyslexic girl once. It didn't
work out.
While I was abroad on business, she sent me a
'John Dear' letter.

He: You never cry out when you have an orgasm.
She: You're never *with* me when I have an orgasm!

(*See also* Naughty Boys, Naughty Girls)

UGLIES

Your photographs don't do you justice . . . they
look exactly *like* you!

Look at that face . . . that's what you get for
telling a witch doctor to piss off!

Physically, this man looks like he was designed by
a committee.

When God put the construction of his face out to
tender, the lowest bidder got the job!

This is the one guy who frightens the shit out of
Freddie Kruger.

He was so ugly as a child, his mother used to have to rub raw fish all over his body to get the cat to play with him.

He's got a great head on his shoulders. Of course, it would look much better on a *neck*, but . . .

He once had his photograph taken but the photographer wouldn't develop it . . . he didn't want to be alone with it in the darkroom!

You should see him when his skin trouble flares up . . . he really is a sight for psoriasis!

I met her at a fancy dress party. She was dressed as an old witch.
We got on like a house on fire.
At the end of the evening, I said, 'Take off your mask'.
She said, 'Mask?'

How can I describe her looks?
Can you imagine Yasser Arafat with plaits?!

She's nearly thirty but she has the acne of a fifteen year old!

What a mess she is! She even wears surgical eyelashes!

I'll never forget the first time I saw her – she was peaches and cream. Except for her neck . . . *that* was more like prunes and custard!

The first thing that struck me about her was her beauty spot . . . then I watched as it crawled away!

This is not a pretty woman. Once, a Peeping-Tom reached in and pulled down her blinds.

Her beautician has started talking about euthanasia.

Many times she's tried to get a man, but to no avail . . . maybe she ought to try *wearing* one!

WAFFLE AND SILLY STUFF

Oh give me a home where the buffalo roam, and I'll show you a home full of buffalo shit!

We don't have a burglar alarm . . . just a sign saying, 'Beware: rottweiler bitch with PMT!'

She ran away from home once. Thankfully, several days later, the police found her safe . . . they never did find her, but at least they found her safe.

Today sees the formation of the British Anti-Nepotism Campaign.
The undersigned are pledged to fight nepotism wherever it may appear.
Chairman: Alfred Emerson, Vice Chairman: Alfred Emerson Jr, Hon. Secretary: Mrs Alfred Emerson, Campaign Treasurer: Miss Alfreda Emerson and Special Campaign Assistant: 'Spot' Emerson (bark!) . . . down boy!

Life is what you make it. Until some bugger comes along and makes it worse!

'If at first you don't succeed, failure may just be your thing.' (Milton Berle)

Three burning political questions . . .
Number one: What's Tony Blair doing in the Labour Party?
Number two: What's Edward Heath doing in the Conservative Party?
Number three: What's Paddy Ashdown *doing*?

If by moving the clocks forward, we keep the sun up one hour longer, why don't we move the clocks forward twelve hours and keep the sun up for ever?!

Today we celebrate 'The Miracle of Virgin' . . . the day Richard Branson walked on the Perrier.

Scientists have announced a new breakthrough; they've successfully crossed a chicken with a hyena . . . it lays an egg, then falls about laughing.

People who live in glasshouses . . . should use the toilet down at the pub.

My mother would be so proud . . . I go to my psychoanalyst twice a week and all we do is talk about her.

When geese listen to horror stories, do they get people-pimples?!

WEDDINGS

GENERAL

In case any of you have arrived late, allow me to bring you up to speed.
We're here this afternoon, to celebrate the marriage of . . . in the blue corner – so far, undefeated – the blushing bride Lucille Patricia and . . . in the red corner – the brave challenger – the *flush*ing bridegroom, David Michael Newberry.

Earlier on, at the ceremony, the sentence was
pronounced.
Now comes the trial!

Marriage is an institution.
Marriage is love.
Love is blind.
Therefore, marriage is an institution for the blind.

'Marriage is punishment for shoplifting in some
countries.'   ('Wayne's World')

When it comes to relationships – love is the quest,
seduction the conquest, and marriage . . . the
inquest.

I think they *should* allow priests to marry . . .
that way, they'd know what Hell really is!

ADVICE TO THE BRIDEGROOM

You have to realise, as a man, that in any
marriage there can only ever be one boss.
So do exactly as she tells you, and you'll be fine.

To keep your marriage brimming in the ever-
loving cup – whenever you're wrong, admit it . . .
whenever you're right, shut up!

There are three things you must remember to give during a marriage: inspiration, income, in.

Behind every successful man is an astonished mother-in-law!

By the way, I have some bad news for you Dave . . . one of the waiters just brought Lucy a couple of aspirins.

ADVICE TO THE BRIDE

Treat him like a dog; three meals a day, plenty of affection and a loose leash.

If he ever threatens to leave you, hold out for a firm promise!

ADVICE TO THE HAPPY COUPLE

As the two of you go forward hand in hand into the big, wide world, I can do no better than offer you some of the advice that has been passed down in our family from generation to generation . . . and never used.

Never do anything in bed that you can't pronounce.

LINES FOR THE BRIDE'S FATHER

You may not have realised this, but the traditional function of the bride's father's speech is to prevent his daughter from having to face her wedding night before she's been properly sedated.

The truth behind this marriage is quite simple. About a year ago, I was working out the family budget and I suddenly realised . . . one of us would have to go.
I chose Lucy.

Lucy told me, the only regret she has about getting married is leaving her mother.
I said, 'No problem darling, take her with you . . . please.'

Today, my sin-in-law becomes my son-in-law.

LINES FOR THE BRIDEGROOM

I feel a bit queasy this afternoon; it must be something I married!

I think I'm beginning to understand how Eurosceptics feel about relinquishing power.

My thanks to our excellent ushers . . . no ceremony was ever better 'ushed'.

Lucy has all that any woman could possibly want . . . me!

Mother-in-Laws are like seeds . . . you don't need them, but they come with the tomato!

Here's to my mother-in-law's daughter,
And here's to her father-in-law's son;
And here's to the vows we've just taken,
And the life we've just begun.

THE SERIAL BRIDE

Poor girl . . . three times a bride, never a bridesmaid.

She's been up and down the aisle more often than Oprah Winfrey!

THE SERIAL BRIDEGROOM

He's walked down the aisle so often, they've sent him the bill for a new carpet!

He's getting married yet again, but this time it's the real thing . . . sex!

He's been married so many times, he's got ingrowing confetti!

Barry is currently enjoying a new lease of wife.

They don't issue him with a new wedding licence any more; they just punch the old one.

He enjoyed his last wedding so much, he can hardly wait till the next one!

His mother was delighted to hear he was getting married . . . mind you, she always is.

This guy's in the habit of crossing his fingers when he takes his wedding vows!

He signs his marriage certificate in pencil!

LINES FOR THE BEST MAN

A little advice, if I may be permitted. It's usually all right to refer to the bridegroom as being a bit of a lad before he met Lucy, but don't mention any specific previous relationships.

Another thing – don't make jokes against the bride. Even if *you* don't suffer as a result, the bridegroom certainly will.

Today I feel very happy and very relieved . . . it's always a relief to be at a wedding that isn't your own.

No, I'm not married myself, but I'm sure the right girl is just around the corner . . . unless the police have moved her on since last night!

I often think about marriage . . . it keeps my mind off sex.

I'm still young enough to want to find a woman to have my children, because frankly . . . I'm pissed off with them!

Lucy has a thing about frogs; she's been collecting them for years . . . but she got so tired of waiting for one of them to turn into a prince, she married him anyway!

Lucy adores animals . . . especially cats. She's totally devoted to a stray she picked up some time ago . . .
but more about Dave a little later.

LINES FOR THE BRIDE

'Some women get all excited about nothing . . . and then marry him.'   (Goldie Hawn)

Women have a higher threshold of pain – and when they get married, men carry them over it.

A few of us girls formed an organisation called 'Marriage Anonymous'. When any of us felt like getting married, the others would send over a surly, balding man with stubble and a beer belly.

THE MATURE COUPLE

They're getting married so late in life . . . the National Health is paying for their honeymoon.

'Something old, something new, something borrowed, something blue'. I don't think there's any doubt about the 'something old' she brought to the ceremony . . . the groom!

My specialised book, *Mitch Murray's One-Liners For Weddings*, also published by Foulsham, offers hundreds more funnies, and includes several sample speeches.

JEWISH WEDDINGS

A dramatic highlight of the Jewish wedding service comes after the couple drink a ceremonial glass of wine, and the bridegroom – by tradition – treads on the glass.
This is to celebrate the very last time the poor guy will ever be able to put his foot down again.

Stephanie knows who she is and where she comes from. She never forget her roots.
Nor does her hairdresser.

During her teens and early twenties, Stephanie was just like any other normal single Jewish girl, waiting to meet Dr Right.

Today we remember the timeless words, spoken by a sweet young girl to her new boyfriend in the back row of the Odeon Marble Arch . . . 'That's funny, you don't *feel* Jewish!'

Last June, I went to a really interesting wedding. It was a Jewish/Hindu ceremony.
The bridegroom broke the glass and the bride walked on it!

I'm not saying Danielle had last minute doubts, but it was the first time I'd ever heard a bride promise to 'love, honour and *oy vay*!'

For those of you unfamiliar with Jewish dietary laws and the Kosher tradition, you only have to remember three things:
Jews don't eat pork, they don't eat shellfish and they don't eat retail.

ADVICE TO THE BRIDEGROOM

Never tell her that her chicken soup isn't as good as your mother used to make . . . unless, of course, you happen to look good wearing noodles in your hair.

WIMPS

I wish the meek would hurry up and inherit the earth. Let's face it, the un-meek are really screwing it up.

Most women like to marry a man with spirit . . . it gives them something to break.

Don't let those vows about 'loving' and 'honouring' fool you . . . she just didn't want to make a scene.

Some men may think they boss the house, when all they really do is house the boss!

He used to be a dude, now he's subdued!

Women like quiet men . . . they think they're listening.

He's never been married . . . he's a self-made mouse.

Edwina Currie is campaigning for the EC to adopt 'nagging' as an official language.

What a wimp! Not only was he afraid of the school bully, he ended up marrying her!

He's a man of few words, but then of course, he's married!

I asked him, 'Are you a man or a mouse?' He said, 'Put a piece of cheese down and you'll soon find out!'